Exeter Medieval English Texts & Studies

General Editors : Marion Glasscoe and M. J. Swanton

T0341495

pacem· precor· semp custodi ad gloriā nominis cuī· qd͛ fic
benedicaī in secula· A M E N·

Nos pueri rogamus te magister ut doceas nos loqui latialit
recte quia idiote sumus & corrupte loquimur. Quid uultis
loqui· quid curamus· quid loquamur nisi recta locutio sit
& utilis non anilis aut turpis. Uultis flagellari in discendo·
Carius est nobis flagellari p doctrina quam nescire· Sed scim
te mansuetum esse & nolle inferre plagas nobis nisi cogaris
a nobis· Interrogo te quid mihi loqueris· quid habes operis·
Professus sum monachus & psallam omni die septe sinaxes
& occupatus sum lectionibus & cantu· sed tamen uelle interim
discere sermocinari latina lingua· Quid sciunt isti tui socii·

ÆLFRIC'S COLLOQUY

Edited by

G. N. GARMONSWAY

UNIVERSITY
of
EXETER
PRESS

First published in Methuen's Old English Library,
London, 1939

This revised edition published by University of Exeter, 1991

University of Exeter Press
Reed Hall, Streatham Drive
Exeter EX4 4QR
UK
www.exeterpress.co.uk

Printed digitally since 2003

ISBN 978 085989 098 4

Printed and bound by CPI Group (UK) Ltd, Croydon, CR0 4YY

PREFACE

THERE is little need to offer any explanation for a new and separate edition of Ælfric's *Colloquy*. It is one of the most commonly read texts, it is peculiarly suited to the needs of beginners, and its interest as a document of educational history is well established. The present edition is based upon a careful re-examination of the manuscripts, whilst the introduction and commentary, besides their obvious concern with the text itself, aim at directing students to some of the more general problems of Anglo-Saxon life.

I am grateful to Professor Bruce Dickins for his kindness in reading the proofs, to Professor Paul Barbier for his help in dealing with the *Saliu* crux, and to my wife for assistance in collating the manuscript in the Plantin-Moretus Museum.

G. N. GARMONSWAY

PREFACE TO THIS EDITION

THIS edition incorporates revisions made by the late G. N. Garmonsway prior to his death in 1967. In addition the bibliography has been recast and brought up to date.

M.J.S.

CONTENTS

ABBREVIATIONS

Archiv	(*Herrigs*) *Archiv für das Studium der neueren Sprachen und Litteraturen*
BT	J. Bosworth and T. N. Toller, *An Anglo-Saxon Dictionary*, 1882, 1921
Bülbring	K. D. Bülbring, *Altenglisches Elementarbuch*, 1902
Colloquy	Ælfric's *Colloquy*
EETS	Early English Text Society
ESt	*Englische Studien*
Glossary	Ælfric's *Glossary*
Grammar	Ælfric's *Grammar*
Hoops *Reallex*	J. Hoops (ed.), *Reallexikon der germ. Altertumskunde*
Luick	K. Luick, *Historische Grammatik der engl. Sprache*, Leipzig, 1921
ME	Middle English
NED	*A New English Dictionary*
OE	Old English
Schlemilch	W. Schlemilch, *Beiträge zur Sprache und Orthographie spätaltengl. Sprachdenkmäler der Übergangszeit*, 1914
Sievers(Cook)	E. Sievers, *An Old English Grammar* (3rd ed.), trans. and ed. A. S. Cook, 1903
Stevenson	W. H. Stevenson, *Early Scholastic Colloquies*, Anecdota Oxoniensia : Mediaeval and Modern Series, part 15, 1929
WSax	West Saxon
Wright-Wülcker	T. Wright, *Anglo-Saxon and Old English Vocabularies*, I (2nd ed.), ed. and collated R. P. Wülcker, 1884
ZfdA	*Zeitschrift für deutsches Altertum*

INTRODUCTION

Ælfric's *Colloquy*, a dialogue between a schoolmaster and his pupils, is one of the earliest English educational documents. Such colloquies had long been used in the monastic schools of Western Europe for the purpose of instruction, and particularly as a device for teaching boys Latin.[1] It was characteristic of the genius of Ælfric that he was able to impart liveliness and spontaneity to the dialogue of his questionnaire, which in the hands of others was rarely free from the tedium of the average academic exercise. To-day the work is chiefly of interest for the picture it presents of the life and activities of the middle and lower classes of Anglo-Saxon society, concerning which Old English literature is, in the main, silent.

I. Versions of Ælfric's *Colloquy*

The Latin version of the *Colloquy* is preserved, either in part or complete, in four manuscripts[2]:

C : British Museum, Cotton MS Tiberius A. iii, fols. 60b–64b.

J : St. John's College, Oxford, Codex No. 154, fols. 204a–221b.

R₁ : Plantin-Moretus Museum, Antwerp, Codex No. 47 (earlier numberings, 32 and 68), fols. 18a–19b.

R₂ : British Museum, Add. MS No. 32246, fols. 16b–17b.

[1] As late as the eighteenth century the colloquies of Erasmus were used for this purpose ; e.g., the translation of John Clarke, 1720, ' designed for the use of beginners in the Latin tongue '.

[2] The symbols are those used by Stevenson, 75 ; in the articles of J. Zupitza, ZfdA xxxi. 32, and E. Schröder, ZfdA xli. 283, J is denoted by O. For C, M. Förster, *Anglia* xli. 148, uses T. For description of the contents of MS Tib. A iii, cf M. Förster, Archiv cxxi. 39.

C is the only text [1] which contains a continuous inter-linear gloss in Old English and has the epilogue (318–end). In R_1R_2 there are no glosses : those in J are infrequent, and occur, as a rule, at the places where the text has been augmented by Ælfric Bata, with his filchings from Ælfric's *Glossary*.

It is probable that C was once in the library of Christ Church, Canterbury, and it may have been copied there. An entry (No. 297) in the library catalogue of Henry of Eastry, prior from 1284–1331, reads *Locutio latina glosata Anglice ad instruendos pueros* (cf. M. R. James, *The Ancient Libraries of Canterbury and Dover*, Cambridge 1903, 50) ; if this describes a text, as is probable (M. Förster, Anglia xli. 147, note 3), then it may well be C.[2] It is possible that it may have been introduced into the school by Æðelnoð, who was Dean of Christ Church and Archbishop from 1020 until his death in 1038 : he was the son of Æðelmær, the founder of the monastery of Cernel in Dorset, and had most likely been a pupil of Ælfric there. Yet the reputation of the *Colloquy* was no doubt so well established in the eleventh century as to make it an inevitable choice for the syllabuses of monastic schools.

The Oxford codex, in which J occurs, is described by W. M. Lindsay (Stevenson, viii). It dates from the early eleventh century, and formerly belonged to the monastery at Durham. It contains Ælfric's *Grammar*, three original colloquies of Ælfric Bata, and J, his elaboration of Ælfric's

---

[1] For a convenient facsimile of C (fol. 61b), cf. H. D. Traill and J. S. Mann, *Social England* (Illustrated Edition), London, 1903, I. 189.

[2] No. 296 in the Catalogue (James, *op. cit.* 50) has the titles of the first three and last text written in the first hand of the Codex, no doubt to indicate everything contained up to fol. 56, where the first hand ends. No. 297 has 10 titles, the description *Locutio . . . pueros* being the second entry. There is no notice in the Catalogue of the text which precedes the *Colloquy* and with which the second hand of the Codex begins (fol. 57a) : the first entry sub No. 297 is *Expositiones de Prisciano exposite Anglice*, whereas the text preceding the *Colloquy* is an office for vespers on All Saints' Day.

Colloquy. J opens with the rubric HANC SENTENTIAM
LATINI SERMONIS OLIM ÆLFRICUS ABBAS COMPOSUIT QUI
MEUS FUIT MAGISTER sed tamen ego Ælfric Bata multas
POSTEA huic ADDIDI APPENDICES.

R_1R_2 contain only portions of the *Colloquy*: R_1 runs
from the beginning to *utimini* 184; R_2 from 185, opening
with *Int* (i.e. *Interrogatio*) *tu*, and ending before the words
et cantaui 269. R_1R_2 were originally written in the outer
margins of several pages of a manuscript of 74 folios which
contained a text of Priscian's Latin Grammar, under the
title *Incipiunt excerptiones de Prisciano*, and on the last
two folios a short Latin glossary, a Latin letter to a priest
Ælf (? Ælfric) and four short pieces of Latin verse. Preceding R_1R_2, and also written in the margins, were an
alphabetical Latin glossary, a Latin-English glossary and
a commentary on the Grammar of Donatus. Part of
the manuscript was copied by Franciscus Junius (Junius
MS 71); in particular the Latin-English glosses (Wright-
Wülcker I. 104–91). M. Förster, Anglia xli. 155 ff, shows
good reason for doubting that the manuscript was ever in
the possession of Rubens, as had been generally stated since
Wanley's description of it as *ex membranis Rubenii Ant-
werpiani*. Subsequent to 1640 (Förster, *op. cit.* 157), 24
leaves were lost from various places in the manuscript;
in 1884 these came into the possession of the British
Museum (Add. MSS 32246); cf E. M. Thompson, *The
Journal of the British Archaeological Association* xli. 144 ff.
Two of these lost leaves contained R_2. Förster, *op. cit.*,
has described the Antwerp manuscript in detail and shown
how its pagination is to be restored.

C is the text of the present edition. Each leaf of the
manuscript is approximately $7'' \times 9\frac{3}{4}''$, with 23 lines to
the page. Down the sides and across the top and bottom
of the writing run two parallel lines. The inner line en-
closes the writing on the left, but on the right of the page
it frequently overflows. The first line of each page is
written above the outer parallel line, and the last between
the parallel lines. Occasionally lines have been drawn across

the page to guide the writing of the Latin. The margin is widest (1¼″) at the bottom of the page.

The Latin text begins on line 6 of fol. 60b with a large capital N, standing out in the space formed by the vertical parallels. It is written continuously until line 16 of fol. 64b, which contains only the words *cum uirga*. Line 17 begins the 'epilogue', which is introduced by the large capital O, similarly placed between the parallels. The punctuation is fairly consistent:

√ is used frequently for the question mark,
; rarely for the full stop,
· frequently for the full stop, sometimes for the comma.

The handwriting of C suggests the second quarter of the eleventh century. Whereas the Latin uses the foreign minuscules of the Carolingian type, the Old English is more conservative, using the flat-topped ʒ and flattened *a* but no longer high *e*. The Old English *y* is dotted, and only the insular forms of *s* are used, high *s* being almost universal : þ is preferred in all positions, ð occurs 12 times, usually finally, never initially : rarely does *r* occur without the long Old English descender. The Old English was probably copied from another glossed version[1] of the *Colloquy* and possibly not by the same scribe as the Latin.

In the present edition no attempt has been made to reproduce the exact positioning of the glosses, although spaces have been left in the Old English to indicate places where words in the Latin stand unglossed. Nor is any indication given of the separation of parts of the same

---

[1] It might be responsible for some of the gross errors of C (e.g. *cræfst* 175, *scræfte* 182, *fræfte* 235 which was, however, corrected) : in 99, 204 the errors are those a copyist is likely to make. Since the *Colloquy* is an exercise in conversation, it is remotely possible that the Old English was originally written in by an advanced pupil during the lesson and that this accounts for 'dictation' errors. It is not likely that the *pueri* themselves were allowed pen and parchment at this early stage in their studies. The beginner learnt to write on wax tablets with a style. Cf. J. B. Mullinger, *The Schools of Charles the Great* (1877) 131.

word : such divisions are not frequent, despite the exigencies of space for the glossator.

II. AUTHORSHIP

C was first described by Wanley (*Catalogues* 1705, 196, art. xxvii) [1] as ' Colloquium ad pueros linguae Latinae locutione exercendos, ab Ælfrico primum compilatum et deinde ab Ælfrico Bata ejus discipulo auctum. Latine et Saxonice '. The beginning and end of the *Colloquy* is then quoted, with the comment ' Post haec fortasse desunt quaedam '. The first part of this description, however, was subsequently misunderstood [2] and gave rise to one of the several misconceptions which have grown around the *Colloquy* and its literary history. Thorpe in both editions of his *Analecta Anglo-Saxonica*, 1834 (101), 1846 (18), set Wanley's description at the head of his text, giving the impression that the words are to be found in the manuscript. In the edition of T. Wright [3] the words reappeared under the title ' The Colloquy of Archbishop [4] Alfric of the Tenth Century ', and misleadingly referred to in a footnote as ' the Latin title '. The assumption that Ælfric's pupil, Bata, had been responsible for the C text led Wright

[1] Cf. also the description by J. Planta, *Catalogue of MSS in the Cottonian Library* 31.

[2] Cf. J. Zupitza, *Die ursprüngliche Gestalt von Ælfrics Colloquium*, ZfdA xxxi. 32 ff.

[3] *Anglo-Saxon and Old English Vocabularies* I. 89 (1857). In the second edition (revised by R. P. Wülcker, 1884), the words remain, again with no indication of their origin. L. F. Klipstein, *Analecta Anglo-Saxonica* (1849) I. 195 ff, following Thorpe, says ' the title found at the head of this article is from the Cottonian MS '.

[4] The *Colloquy* was frequently ascribed to Archbishop Ælfric (d. 1005) by early editors, and the ascription has reappeared in M. Anderson and B. C. Williams, *Old English Handbook* (Boston 1935) 144. Wülcker, *Preface* ii, drew attention to the ' mistake which had slipped into the superscription ' in Wright's edition. E. Dietrich, *Zeitschrift für die Historische Theologie* xxvi. 199 ff, had shown that the identification of Ælfric the author with Archbishop Ælfric was untenable ; and Wharton, in England, as early as 1691 had already disproved it (*Anglia Sacra* I. 125 ff). Cf. C. L. White, *Ælfric* (*Yale Studies in English* 2), cap. vii.

to the erroneous conclusion [1] that 'the enlarged edition of the colloquy, by Alfric Bata, seems to have so entirely superseded the original, that it appears to be the only one now preserved . . . the only other copy known is preserved in the Library of St. John's College, Oxford'. The correct interpretation of the facts had meanwhile been set forth by Dietrich, *op. cit.* xxv. 492, 525 (note 82), and Ten Brink,[2] who seeing that J contained many amplifications which were absent from C, concluded that C was nearer to and might well be Ælfric's original version, the new material in J representing the elaborations of Bata to which Wanley had referred. Zupitza, *op. cit.* 32 ff, subsequently discussed the relationship and dependence of the two texts, and Schröder [3] showed in detail how most of the additions [4] in J had been purloined, with little discrimination, from Ælfric's *Glossary*. It is now generally agreed that the C text is the nearest approach we have to Ælfric's original. The texts R_1R_2 appear to stand closer to C than to J : they contain none of the catalogues of J, and many of the shorter additions to J, which are absent from C, are also absent from R_1R_2. These fragmentary texts are chiefly interesting for the 'stage directions'[5]

[1] Re-echoed by Lindsay, *op. cit.* vi, 'it is unfortunate that we have not Ælfric's *Colloquy* in its original form, but only as enlarged by his pupil, Ælfric Bata, who, in enlarging, marred it sadly'.

[2] *Early English Literature* (trans. H. M. Kennedy, 1883) I. 107

[3] E. Schröder, *Colloquium Ælfrici*, ZfdA xli. 283 ff.

[4] J keeps the sentence framework of C, but Ælfric's direct conversational style is elaborated by the addition of adjectives, adverbs and otiose expressions, often alliterative and rhetorical. Bata's hand is most apparent in the pedantic lists of words which swell out the answers. E.g. after *uarie bestie* 78, comes the phrase in J *et uermes atque animalia, bona ac mala, munda et inmunda, morantur in siluis* : then a new question *Et quae ?* answered by a list of about 50 animals, many of them foreign beasts. Bata's own colloquies (cf Stevenson 26 ff) show how this pedantry must have destroyed all the virtues of this form of instruction. Lindsay, *op. cit.* vii, says ' we must write down Aelfric Bata with Dogberry '.

[5] At 4, R_1 has the letter R (for *Responsio*) before *Quid uultis loqui ?* : before 7, the letter M (for *Magister*) ; before 8, D (for *Discipuli*), &c. No such directions appear in C before 194 *Dicit cocus,*

they contain, which are not present in the first part of C, and which are also absent from many places in J.

There seems to be no need to doubt the assertion of Bata that Ælfric was the author of the *Colloquy*, since Bata [1] may have been an oblate at Eynsham during the time that his *magister* was abbot there, i.e. after 1005. Moreover, the work forms a natural sequel, as a practical exercise, to the *Grammar* and *Glossary*, which were probably composed during the time that he was master of the oblates at Cernel (White, *op. cit.* 47 ff). Schröder, *op. cit.* 284, says ' the arrangement of the *Glossary* is presupposed in the *Colloquy*, for example in the choice of certain groups of words, such as the names of animals and fishes ' Moreover, the *Grammar* actually contains brief conversa-

whereafter they are frequent. It would be rash to assume this has any significance : if there be any question of an addition to the *Colloquy* it will be the section 203 ff, where new characters are introduced, and to deny this to Ælfric would rob him of the best scene in the piece. The epilogue 308 ff may well not be Ælfric's : such general remarks on conduct could well have been added by any one wishing to enlarge on the Benedictine Rule (e.g. ' scurrilities, or idle words, or words which move to laughter, in any part of the monastery, we condemn by a perpetual prohibition ') and are in fact common (cf. 314 note). Wanley had every reason for supposing that there was more of this kind of epilogue.

[1] Apart from the rubric of J, all we know of Bata is derived from *Osberni Vita Dunstani*, written in the time of Lanfranc (*Memorials of St. Dunstan* (Rolls Series, 1874) 136 ; cf. *Eadmeri Vita Dunstani, ibid.*, 227). Here the story is told of how Dunstan appeared in a vision to one who had sought his shrine to be cured, apologizing for not being able to attend to his case sooner as he had been busy dealing with Ælfric Bata, who had tried to disinherit the Church of God (*nam ecclesiam Dei Alfricus, cognomento Bata, exhaeredare temptavit, sed me tutore nihil efficere potuit*). As White, *op. cit.* 122 note, says, this suggests that Bata was living after the Conquest, and hence was more likely to have been with Ælfric at Eynsham than earlier at Cernel. Cf. also T. Wright, *Biographia Brit. Literaria* 496 ff. One of Bata's original colloquies (Stevenson, 27) has this heading : *Denique composuit pueris hoc stilum rite diuersum, qui Bata Ælfricus monachus breuissimus qualiter scolastici ualeant resumere fandi aliquod initium Latinitatis sibi.*

7

tions [1] which serve as illustrations to grammatical detail.
Ælfric was, of course, familiar with the colloquy form as a
method of instruction, but these snatches of dialogue seem
to be adumbrations of the up-to-date conversation piece
he was ultimately to compose for his pupils. We need not,
obviously, assume the direct dependence [2] of the *Colloquy*
on either the *Grammar* or *Glossary*, such as we find when
Bata goes to work, for it is obvious that a man of Ælfric's
ability would be able to dispense with his word-lists : in
fact, the first version may well have been a brief extem-
pore [3] creation while he was taking a class, with the addition
of new material as the pupils progressed and extended their
vocabulary : it is possible that many and varied versions
were once in use before any one was written down. The
Latin of C may originally have been written down [4] by
Ælfric ; we cannot say more than that it represents one
of the many possible variations of it which he may have
had in use.

It is a more difficult question to decide the authorship

[1] Cf. e.g. J. Zupitza, *Ælfrics Grammatik und Glossar* (1880) 22 ;
to illustrate the use of the dative the following occurs : ' *Huic
homini do equum* ' ; ' *Quid das mihi* ' ? ' *Unum librum do.*' Or
again, *ʒif þu cpest nu,* ' *hpa lærde ðe* ? ', *þonne cpeðe ic,* ' *Dunstan* '.
' *Hpa hadode ðe* ? '. ' *He me hadode.*'

[2] Indeed, if the *Glossary* was ' set ' to prepare the boys for the
test of the *Colloquy*, then the *pueri* might well have complained
that the questions asked were ' outside the scope of the syllabus '.
But apparently they are so well prepared that they declare themselves ready to debate any topic (5). We may suspect that Ælfric
had many such word-lists in use, and that the *Colloquy* was built
round one which has not been preserved.

[3] The spontaneity of the earlier parts suggests this : the section
237–65 especially, with its rhetorical effects and alliteration, is
more bookish and studied.

[4] The absence of any preface, unlike his usual practice, may
suggest that Ælfric was not the scribe of the first draft : even the
Glossary, which unlike the *Grammar* has no preface, has the per-
sonal touch at the end *Þe ne maʒan spa þeah ealle naman apritan
ne furþon ʒeþencan.* The absence of any particular directions how
the *Colloquy* was to be used in class is of no significance : such
usage, whatever it may have been, was no doubt too well established to need explanation.

8

of the Old English interlinear gloss which appears in C. Opinions have varied as to Ælfric's authorship, but the view of most scholars that it is not likely to be his probably best accords with the facts and with the results of the unsatisfactory tests which can be made. It is hardly likely that a scholar of Ælfric's standing would need to add glosses for his own use. As Wright, *op. cit.* vii, says of the vocabularies ' in the earlier and better period, no doubt the teacher had such lists merely in Latin, or glossed [1] only in cases of difficulty, and he was sufficiently learned in the language to explain them himself '. Yet if the Latin version was written out by Ælfric for use by others in his own monastery, or to be circulated to other foundations, we can imagine that he would take care to furnish it with an Old English gloss, knowing all too well the ignorance of the Latin tongue displayed by clerics of his time : it will be remembered in this connexion that most of his other works have prefaces in both Latin and the vernacular. On the other hand, it has been frequently pointed out that the glosses show, in places, a surprising ignorance [2] of the Latin, which critics have been unwilling [3] to ascribe to Ælfric. Another argument against his authorship is Schröder's, who points out (*op. cit.* 289) that many of the Old English words are not those used in the *Glossary* to define the same Latin words. He instances the following [4] :

[1] Sometimes in code, when ' the usual system . . . consists of substituting for every vowel the following consonant ' (J. M. Clark, *The Abbey of St. Gall* (1926) 107 f). Professor Bruce Dickins points out the use of cipher in a Latin distich in Cott. Titus D xxvi. (cf. W. de G. Birch, *Liber Vitae* (Hampshire Record Society, 1892) 275.)

[2] Originally pointed out by Wright, *op. cit* vii. note.

[3] Yet Zupitza, *Ælfrics Grammatik*, Preface, takes the standpoint ' fehler der hs. . . . habe ich dann unverbessert gelassen, wenn mir die möglichkeit nicht ausgeschlossen schien, dass sich Ælfric selbst geirrt haben könnte '.

[4] Other interesting examples are edax *uel* glutto, *paxjeorn* (*Coll.*) *oferetol* (*Gloss.*) ; sacerdos, *mæssepreost* (*Coll.*) *sacerd* (*Gloss.*) ; murenas, *lampredan* (*Coll.*) *merenæddre* (*Gloss.*) ; tracta, *sceota* (*Coll.*) *truht* (*Gloss.*). Schröder is wrong, however, in saying that *þræl* glosses *servus*. Cf. 201 note.

	Colloquy	Glossary
consiliarius	ʒeþeahta	rædbora
	ʒeþeahtend	
ferrarius	isenesmiþ	isenpyrhta
aerarius	arsmiþ	mæstlinʒsmið
servus	þræl	ðeopa
sutor	sceopyrhta	sutere

Although he is much too sanguine in supposing that this
list could be extended ' a hundredfold ', it is true that
many such variations exist.[1] Yet it is possible that
Schröder has not realized that the English words in the
Glossary are for the child, and those in the *Colloquy* are
for the master, who alone has a copy of the text. In the
Glossary the child is taught,[2] *sutor þæt is sutere*, and in
so far as *sutere* conveys to his mind the meaning of *sutor*,
that is sufficient : the aim is not to extend the child's
vernacular but to provide him with a Latin vocabulary,
and the English word is but ancillary to that end. The
master, on the other hand, may gloss his text as he pleases
when he prepares the *Colloquy* to take in class : he will
have no compunction in writing *sceopyrhta* above *sutor*, if
it occurs to him first. It is probably correct, however, to
assume that Ælfric would make the glosses of the *Glossary*
and *Colloquy* correspond, but that subsequent masters and
scribes might well depart here and there from the set terms
of the *Glossary* in making a translation for their own use.

[1] If the gloss is Ælfric's, the correspondence might be expected
to be close, not only on the ground of common authorship but also
because he was alive to the necessity for straightforward methods
in instructing young children, and would be likely, for this reason,
to prefer to make the English equivalents to the Latin tally in
both *Colloquy* and *Glossary* (cf. *Grammar*, Latin Preface, *sed ego
deputo hanc lectionem inscientibus puerulis, non senibus, aptandam
fore. Scio multimodis uerba posse interpretari, sed ego simplicem
interpretationem sequor fastidii uitandi causa*).

[2] The glosses were probably given out by the master and, in the
early stages, memorized by repetition ; at later stages copied on
to wax tablets and memorized therefrom. The colloquy is an
exercise built upon the vocabulary so learnt, the aim being to
converse in Latin without promptings in the vernacular.

In stressing these differences the resemblances must not be overlooked, for the English of a large proportion of the technical words agrees with that of the *Glossary*, while most of the rest of the vocabulary [1] can be paralleled in the other works of Ælfric, although no doubt in common use in the monastic schools of the time. From the style of the Old English no conclusions can be drawn ; its character is largely conditioned by the mechanical methods of the glossator, which are responsible for many of the crudities and unnatural rhythms that occur. The final impression is that the Old English version is not by Ælfric, but was added later [2] by another teacher : the main gaps in the gloss occur, as might be expected, over oft-repeated phrases and words where the master felt he could trust to his memory or refresh it by reference to a previous page.

III. MASTER AND PUPIL

The education [3] of the oblate in a monastic house was based on the *artes liberales* of the Romans, and made

[1] For examinations of Ælfric's vocabulary cf. *inter alia* G. E. MacLean, *Anglia* vi. 468 ff, S. J. Crawford, *Exameron Anglice* 24 ff, K. Jost, *Anglia* li. 183 ff. Jost prepares a list of test words and tries to determine, by their absence or presence in a text, whether Ælfric was the author. The list, as applied to the *Colloquy*, gave no results, owing to the infrequent appearance of the particular words. E.g. in support of Ælfric's authorship, the appearance of *yrðlinȝ* (vice *eorðtilia*), *ȝereord* (v. *ȝepeode*), *ætforan* (v. *beforan*) : against Ælfric, *ceaster, ceasterpara* (v. *burh, burhpara*), *onfon* (v. *underfon*). In view of the fact that most writers acknowledge Ælfric's large vocabulary and versatility of expression, this method of investigation is not satisfactory.

[2] Schröder, *op. cit.* 290, suggests, without explanation, that the character of the vocabulary makes it probable that the gloss was added one or two generations later.

[3] Cf. Charlemagne's *Admonitio Generalis* (789), *Et ut scolae legentium puerorum-fiant. Psalmos, notas, cantus, compotum, grammaticam per singula monasteria uel episcopia et libros catholicos bene emendate* (Mon. Germ. Hist. II. i. 60). For accounts of the mediæval curriculum, see F. A. Specht, *Geschichte des Unterrichtswesens in Deutschland* (Stuttgart 1885) ; J. Evans, *Monastic Life at Cluny* (Cambridge 1927); J. M. Clark, *op. cit.* 91 ff.

provision for instruction in seven subjects: Grammar, Rhetoric, Dialectic, Music, Arithmetic, Geometry and Astronomy. Long before the first three, the 'trivium', could be begun, the novices' studies were of a more elementary character. They were first taught the letters of the alphabet, the words of the *credo* and *paternoster*: in course of time, by repeating the psalms after the master, they would have the whole Psalter by heart. At the same time they were engaged in learning the settings for the chants [1] used in the canonical office, so that they could join the brethren in the services of the day; some of the antiphons and responsories were sung by the boys alone during the service. Instruction was also given, during these preliminary years, in the three *R*'s and in the elements of Latin grammar. The first reading book was the Psalter, with the words of which the boys were already familiar. Ælfric's *Colloquy* was composed for a class at this elementary [2] stage. In addition to its obvious value for instruction in Latin grammar and syntax, its purpose was to teach the boys correct pronunciation and clear enunciation; 'their aim was to read Latin, write Latin, and dispute in Latin'.[3] The Benedictine Rule, observed in Saxon monasteries, was particularly strict about precise articulation,[4]

[1] It was their duty to begin the chant of grace at meals 'unless they were hoarse, when the precentor shall begin' (G. G. Coulton, *Five Centuries of Religion* (Cambridge 1923) I. 226.

[2] E. Merrill, *The Dialogue in English Literature* (*Yale Studies in English* 42, 1911) 21, in speaking of the elucidaries says, 'they merely use the method of dialogue for exposition of the most technical sort', and adds, strangely, 'this is true of Ælfric's *Colloquy*'. Cf. E. E. Wardale, *Chapters on Old English Literature* 268.

[3] R. W. Chambers, *Thomas More* 58. At the school of St. Gall, towards the end of the tenth century, none of the boys, except the smallest, were allowed to speak to their fellow pupils in any other language but Latin (Specht, *op. cit.* 77): although this would be the ideal aimed at, we have no evidence to show this was enforced in English schools. Cf., however, F. A. Gasquet, *The Old English Bible* (1908) 241.

[4] Cf. Benedictine Rule, cap. xlv. *De his qui falluntur in oratorio.* That the monks themselves were not free from such faults may be gathered from the story of the devil Tutivillius, who is 'specially

and when the boys joined in the services and acted in turn as *lector* at meals, mistakes in chanting or in reading were regarded as unpardonable blunders and punished severely. It is small wonder that the boys, in the *Colloquy*, ask to be taught to speak Latin *recte* and care little for the subject of conversation. Since, both in and out of school, they were supposed to avoid the vernacular, it was necessary to provide them with an adequate vocabulary, not only of bookish terms but also of words of everyday use.[1] For this purpose lists of words, with their English equivalents,[2] were drawn up, classified under various headings, e.g. *De Instrumentis Agricolarum, Nomina Ferarum*, and the pupils committed them to memory. Such in fact was Ælfric's *Glossary*, drawn up to form an appendix to his *Grammar*, and used in the classroom. ' But the genial master, author of the earliest grammar of medieval Europe, made this task easy and pleasant for his pupils. He assigned to each a rôle suitable to the section learned for the day and

deputed to collect the fragments of speech which drop from " dangling, leaping, dragging, mumbling, fore-skipping, fore-running, and overleaping monks " ' (Coulton, *op. cit.* I. 88).

[1] This is in the tradition of the earliest colloquies for learning Greek. Cf. Lindsay, *op. cit.* Introd., where reference is made to a colloquy containing ' a bilingual description of daily doings ' : *mane surgo. Vesti me ; da mihi calciamenta et udones et braccas. Iam calceatus sum ; adfer aquam manibus.* Cf. Foster Watson, *The English Grammar Schools* 342, for similar methods in the sixteenth century.

[2] These vocabularies derive ultimately from the *Hermeneumata Pseudo-Dositheana*, a manual composed about A.D. 200 for the use of Greeks studying Latin or for Latin speakers studying Greek. It contains a list of Greek words with their Latin equivalents : in another section is a bilingual description of the daily life of the schoolboy (cf. Lindsay, *op. cit.* v.). An interesting Old English vocabulary found at St. Gall, is described by Clark, *op. cit.* 69 : ' there are no lists of specifically learned expressions, not even theological terms. The gloss is composed of words drawn from various spheres of daily life : man in relation with his fellows, his attributes, parts of the human body, the sky and the weather, time, the earth, the dwellings of men, the materials from which houses are built, trees, animals and birds.'

catechized [1] them . . . what an admirable way of instructing boys in Latin vocabulary.' [2] In the first stages he no doubt suggested specimen answers, much as he does in the *Grammar*, but his aim was to encourage his pupils to frame their own replies,[3] based on their own observation of the manifold activities of a monastic house.[4] It may well be that the *Colloquy* contains some of the best of these replies, edited by Ælfric himself.

The *Colloquy*, which flowers so unexpectedly from the heavy soil of the glossaries, has often been culled by economists, educationalists, and social historians to brighten the early pages of their histories. But so convincing and realistic is the dialogue that many of them have misunderstood its origin and plan, and have imagined that the class for which it was intended was actually composed of the characters who take part in the discussion. They speak of the ploughman, smith, merchant, &c., as pupils in the monastic school and imagine each to be recounting his experiences. For example, A. F. Leach, *Educational Charters and Documents* [5] xvi, says, ' if it really represents

---

[1] In Ælfric's *Colloquy* the teacher asks the questions and directs the course of the discussion, but the pupils do most of the talking, and at 220 ff take the discussion entirely into their own hands. In this respect it differs from the colloquies of Alcuin, Richalm, Caesarius, or the *Elucidaria*, where the novice seeks information from the teacher. In many of these the author is merely using the dialogue-form as a convenient framework for his treatise. Bata, who imitates Ælfric, stultifies his purpose by talking too much and by brow-beating his pupils (cf. Stevenson 51 f).

[2] Lindsay, *op. cit.* vi., seems to have been the first English writer to understand that this was the procedure in the *Colloquy*, although it had been clearly stated by Schröder, *op. cit.* 283.

[3] e.g. the ingenuous remarks (279 ff) were surely unrehearsed.

[4] Most monasteries were self-sufficing : the kitchens, granges, workshops, &c., must have had a great attraction for the young boys. For the organization of a Benedictine house, v. R. H. Snape, *English Monastic Finances in the Later Middle Ages* (Cambridge 1926) 13, Evans, *op. cit.* 67, 84.

[5] Again in his *Schools of Medieval England* 91, ' the master himself is obviously a secular . . . not acquainted with the secrets of monastic life, while the school is clearly not in the monastery, and

English schools at the time it shows an amazing diffusion of education among all classes, boys in all the different occupations, ploughboy, gamekeeper . . . merchant, learning Latin of a secular master side by side with a young monk.' The difficulties [1] which beset such views are many and are rarely faced by their authors, who have not realized the implicit dependence of the *Colloquy* upon the wordlists : indeed, it is significant that Lindsay, whose main interest was in the mediæval glossaries, should have been almost the first to state the procedure correctly. It is, in fact, Ælfric's genius as a teacher which alone ensures the verisimilitude of the *Colloquy* : there is no reason why it should not have contained much fantastic and extraneous matter built upon recondite glossary words, such as we find in Bata, which would have rendered it worthless as a mirror of English life before the Conquest.

IV. Language

The interlinear gloss may be regarded as an example of the speech common in English schools towards the close

the boys are lay folk drawn from all ranks and occupations . . . not the school of a village like Eynsham, but of a great city like Winchester, which . . . was one of the chief resorts of merchants, and, as a great port, of seamen also '. Cf. for similar misconceptions, W. Cunningham, *Growth of English Industry and Commerce* I. 131 ; A Cruse, *The Shaping of English Literature* 70 ; G. G. Coulton, *Social Life in Britain* 54. Often the facts are stated ambiguously (e.g. *The Cambridge History of English Literature* I. 119).

[1] e.g. the class is addressed as *pueri*, and treated as such in class and in dormitory : one can hardly imagine a merchant, who might be ȝesiðcund, putting up with such treatment. Is there any evidence to show that bondmen were ever admitted into the monastery school ? The class meets in the cloisters (*claustrum*) and forms the inner school ; lay scholars, if any, were always kept apart and taught in a different part of the monastery. From the eleventh century on, day pupils were discouraged (cf. G. G. Coulton, *Medieval Studies* (1913) No. 10, 9 ff). Moreover, the case of Chad (Bede, *Hist. Eccles.* IV. 3) suggests that the Church was wiser than to expect men who had entered the monastery late in life to struggle with their letters. (Cf. the story of ' Our Lady's Tumbler ', Coulton, *op. cit.* I. 371.)

of the Anglo-Saxon period. It exhibits most of the characteristic features of late WSax and of the language of the extant copies of Ælfric's work ; it probably dates from the first half of the eleventh century, judging, *inter alia*, by the obsolescence of the earlier inflexional distinctions and from the prominence of *y* in representing earlier *i*, *y*, and *ie* from many sources, etc. (Luick § 281, Bülbring § 306). The inverted spelling *utpyrpe* 95 suggests a date after 1000, when *weor-* and *wyr-* were levelled under *wur-* (Luick § 286 and Anm. 1).[1] Although unrounding of stable *y*, before palatals or *n*, is found in *bicgean* 301 (it is general in *cinȝce*), *y* usually remains [2] (e.g. *synnum* 314). This may suggest that the gloss was not made in the SW. area (e.g. at Cernel), but the evidence is too slight. The forms *mæniȝe* 119, *ȝepæmmodlice* 3 may possibly be from the S.E. Sax. Pat. (Bülbring § 171), or examples of inverted spelling. The variation of *æ* and *e*, *ȩ* (e.g. *þæs* 48, *hæbbe* 41, &c.) and that of *eo* with *ea* (e.g. *cleafan* 181, *seolmas* 272, *heoldan* 217, *deor* 282), are probably of no significance.[3] Against the fact that the glossator makes frequent mistakes [4] in transcribing, it is interesting to note that he has preserved the only example of the historically correct form *rec(e)an* in *rece* 5 (Sievers § 407, note 12).

The syntax of the OE gloss is conditioned not only by the fact that it is an interlinear gloss, but also by the fact that it was designed for a colloquy, where, in the interest of the *magister*, it was as important to render each Latin word by its English equivalent, as to render the meaning of the sentence as a whole. At the beginning, an attempt is made to supply a full gloss, but in the later

---

[1] There is no trace of the very late change of *wor-*, followed by a vowel, to *wur-*.

[2] Luick, § 281 and Anm. 1. The *Grammar* and *Glossary* show a preponderance of *i* forms in most of the texts.

[3] The unorthodox *leden*, usually found in Ælfric, is the *Colloquy* form. For *ea* for *eo* in Ælfric, cf. Schlemilch, pp. 26, 29.

[4] Although they have been left in the text as remotely possible forms, it would be difficult to substantiate *forlæst* 141, *afest* 137 (Sievers, § 359, 2) ; *ȝefeo* 66 ; *follce* 151 ; *rann* 66, *toȝehyhte* 216.

parts of the *Colloquy* some of the more frequent phrases stand unglossed as if, by then, they needed no further explanation. The natural OE word order is often preferred in short phrases (e.g. *professus sum/ic eom ʒeanpyrde*), but there is no settled practice in rendering some simple combinations (e.g. *uxorem meam et filios meos/min pif 7 minne sunu*), although in general the Latin order is preserved. On the whole there are fewer infelicities (e.g. 134, 117) than might have been expected ; and when they occur, it is due rather to scribal carelessness (e.g. 99), of which there is a good deal in the text, or to misunderstanding of the original (e.g. 146, 164).

ÆLFRIC'S COLLOQUY

(MS Cotton Tiberius A.iii, fols. 60b–64b)

Þe cildra biddaþ þe, eala lareop, þæt þu tæce us
Nos pueri rogamus te, magister, ut doceas nos

sprecan   forþam unʒelærede pe syndon 7
loqui latialiter recte, quia idiote sumus et

ʒepæmmodlice pe sprecaþ.
corrupte loquimur.

Hpæt pille ʒe sprecan ?
Quid uultis loqui ?

Hpæt rece pe hpæt pe sprecan, buton hit riht spræc   **5**
Quid curamus quid loquamur, nisi recta locutio

sy 7 behefe, næs idel oþþe fracod.
sit et utilis, non anilis aut turpis.

Þille bespunʒen on leornunʒe ?
Uultis flagellari in discendo ?

Leofre ys us beon bespunʒen for lare þænne hit
Carius est nobis flagellari pro doctrina quam

TEXTUAL VARIANTS : The capitalization and punctuation have
been modernized in general, but all the MS capitals have been
retained. The following OE contractions have been expanded
without comment : þ(þæt), -ŭ, -ā, -ō (-um, -am, -om), together
with the usual Latin abbreviations.

  ⁶ *behefe*] *behese*   **⁷** *bespunʒen*] *bespuʒen*

---

  ¹ *cildra :* on the pl. with *r*, cf. Sievers(Cook) § 290 note 2.   Gf.
æiʒra **²³⁰**.
  ³ sc. *leden rihte*
  ⁵ *rece pe :* cf Sievers(Cook) § 407 note 12.
  ⁷ On the frequent use of the birch in monastic schools, cf. G. G.
Coulton, *op. cit.* I. 226, 343. For a description, in a colloquy, of
a flogging, v. Stevenson, 62 : cf. the representation of a boy being
handed at a grammar lesson in A. F. Leach, *The Schools of Medieval
England* 88 (from Brit. Mus. MS Burney, 270, fol. 94).

ne cunnan. Ac þe pitun þe bilepitne þesan 7 nellan
  nescire. Sed scimus te mansuetum esse et nolle
onbelæden spincȝla us, buton þu bi toȝenydd fram us. 10
  inferre plagas nobis, nisi cogaris a nobis.
  Ic axie þe, hpæt   sprycst þu? Hpæt hæfst þu
    Interrogo te, quid mihi loqueris? Quid habes
þeorkes?
  operis?
  Ic eom ȝeanpyrde monuc, 7 ic sincȝe ælce dæȝ seofon
    Professus sum monachus, et psallam omni die septem
tida mid ȝebroþrum, 7 ic eom bysȝod   7 on
  sinaxes cum fratribus, et occupatus sum lectionibus et
sanȝe, ac þeahhpæþere ic polde betþenan leornian sprecan 15
    cantu, sed tamen uellem interim discere sermocinari
on leden ȝereorde.
  latina lingua.
  Hpæt cunnon þas þine ȝeferan?
    Quid sciunt isti tui socii?

13 monachus] *monachum*

---

⁹ *pitun :* so Stevenson correctly ; Wright-Wülcker read *pitan.*
Cf. Luick § 326.
¹⁰ *onbelæden :* The inf. in -*en* occurs in *cypen* 164, but here it
may be due to the influence of *læden.*
¹¹ *quid . . . quid :* J has *qui* for the first *quid,* which Zupitza,
op. cit. 40, prefers (cf. 203). Stevenson reads *quid.*
¹³ *dæȝ :* loc. without inflexion (Sievers(Cook) § 237 note 2). Cf.
æt ham 25. *seofon tida :* the seven canonical ' hours ' were the
main services of the monastic day, which aimed at fulfilling the
words of Psalm 119, ' in the midst of the night will I rise to give
thanks to thee . . . seven times a day do I praise thee '. Cf.
G. G. Coulton, *op. cit.* I. 213, 231–2. The times of the services
were : 2 (Matins and Lauds), 6 (Prime and Mass), 9 (Tierce),
12 (Sext), 15 (None), 18 (Vespers), 20 (Compline). There is some
doubt as to the exact times at which sext and none were sung.
Cf. Abbot Butler, *Benedictine Monachism* cap. XVII. A. Hamilton
Thompson, *English Monasteries* 136 ff.
¹⁴ J adds *nimis* before *lectionibus. On sanȝe :* ' nowhere was the
rod used so freely as in the singing class : the pupils had to learn
the complicated system of signs then used in musical notation and
they had to know the melodies by heart ' (Clark, *op. cit.* 99). sc.
on rædinȝa.

Sume synt yrþlincᴣas, sume scephyrdas, sume
Alii sunt aratores, alii opiliones, quidam

oxanhyrdas, sume eac spylce huntan, sume fisceras,
bubulci, quidam etiam uenatores, alii piscatores,

sume fuᴣeleras, ṣume cypmenn, sume scepyrhtan, **20**
alii aucupes, quidam mercatores, quidam sutores,

sealteras, bæceras.
quidam salinatores, quidam pistores, coci.

Hpæt sæᴣest þu, yrþlinᴣc ? Hu beᴣæst þu peorc þin ?
Quid dicis tu, arator ? Quomodo exerces opus tuum ?

Eala, leof hlaford, þearle ic deorfe. Ic ᴣa ut on dæᴣræd
O, mi domine, nimium laboro. Exeo diluculo

þypende oxon to felda, 7 iuᴣie hiᴣ to syl ; nys hit spa
minando boues ad campum, et iungo eos ad aratrum ; non est tam

stearc pinter þæt ic durre lutian æt ham for eᴣe hlafordes **25**
aspera hiems ut audeam latere domi pro timore domini

mines, ac ᴣeiukodan oxan, 7 ᴣefæstnodon sceare 7 cultre
mei, sed iunctis bobus, et confirmato uomere et cultro

mit þære syl, ælce dæᴣ ic sceal erian fulne æcer oþþe mare.
aratro, omni die debeo arare integrum agrum aut plus.

21 *pistores*] altered from *pastores* *coci*] *loci*   **25** *hiems*] *hiemps*
27 *æcer*] *æþer* *arare*] *aratre*

---

18 Cf. *Glossary* (ed. Zupitza, 301-2) for this enumeration.

20 *aucupes : aucipes* J. Cf. *Grammar* (ed. Zupitza, 67) auceps
fuᴣelere, aucipis uel aucupis.

21 pistores, coci. Cf. *pistores quidam quoque coci* J. The cook
follows the baker in the discussion which follows (192).

22 *sæᴣest :* Sievers(Cook) § 416 note 3 : cf. *seᴣst* **111**, *sæᴣst* **112**.

26 *ᴣeiukodan . . . syl :* the two dat. absolutes correspond to the
abl. abs. of the Latin. *ᴣefæstnodon :* dat.pl., to be taken with
both *sceare* and *syl*. ' The share is the iron blade in a plough
which cuts the ground at the bottom of the furrow ; the coulter
the iron blade fixed in front of the share, it cuts the soil vertically '
(NED). Cf. Riddle XXI, and *Pierce the Ploughmans Crede* (ed.
W. W. Skeat) 16, ll. 420 ff. ; also Hoops *Reallex* I. 26, for representation of ploughinᴣ (from Brit. Mus. Cott. Tib. B v. fol. 7b),
also the Luttrell Psalter, fol. 170 (ed. E. G. Millar, London 1932).
Professor Bruce Dickins draws my attention to an interesting
account of ploughing in Lewis which occurs in one of Hogg's letters
(quoted by E. C. Batho, *The Ettrick Shepherd* 47).

27 *æcer :* originally as much land as a yoke of oxen could plough
in a day. Cf. G. B. Grundy, *Essays and Studies* VIII. 38. ' The

Hæfst þu æniȝne ȝeferan?
Habes aliquem socium?

Ic hæbbe sumne cnapan þypende oxan mid ȝadisene,
Habeo quendam puerum minantem boues cum stimulo,

þe eac spilce nu has ys for cylde 7 hreame.
qui etiam modo raucus est pre frigore et clamatione.   **30**

Hpæt mare dest þu on dæȝ?
Quid amplius facis in die?

Ꝺepyslice þænne mare ic do. Ic sceal fyllan binnan
Certe adhuc plus facio. Debeo implere presepia

oxan mid hiȝ, 7 pæterian hiȝ, 7 scearn heora beran ut.
boum feno, et adaquare eos, et fimum eorum portare foras.

Hiȝ! Hiȝ! micel ȝedeorf ys hyt.
O! O! magnus labor.

Ꝺeleof, micel ȝedeorf hit ys, forþam ic neom freoh.   **35**
Etiam, magnus labor est, quia non sum liber.

     sceaphyrde, hæfst þu æniȝ ȝedeorf?
     Quid dicis tu, opilio? Habes tu aliquem laborem?

---

33 pæterian] pæte terian   scearn] sceasn   **34** a third *O* erased
36 laborem] labore

---

long hours of which Ælfric's ploughman complained would not greatly differ from those insisted on in the Act of 1495 ' (Cunningham, *op cit.* I. 391 note 2). Cf. H. S. Bennett, *Life on the English Manor.*

33 *binnan :* this is the only weak form recorded by BT of the usual strong f. *binn(e)* : perhaps the redundant *n* was added because of the assonance of *fyllan binnan oxan.* *Oxan :* gen.pl. (Sievers(Cook) § 276 note 4) or dat.pl.

34 For accounts of what the lord demanded from his servants, cf. G. G. Coulton, *The Medieval Village* 307, and the OE *Be ȝescead-pisan ȝerefa (Anglia* ix. 259; printed, with translation, by Cunningham, *op. cit.* I. 571 ff).

35 ȝeleof : A. J. Wyatt, *An Anglo-Saxon Reader* 40, may be right in altering to ȝea, leof (cf. **37**). *ic neom freoh :* Wright, *op. cit.* 91, says ' this passage is a curious illustration of the feeling of commiseration for the condition of the servile class, which prevailed among the Anglo-Saxon clergy '. The barbarous punishments for slaves which they sanction in the Laws, however, hardly bears this out. Cf. G. G. Coulton, *Social Life in Britain* 336, H. S. Bennett, *op. cit.* 281, on the attitude of the mediæval church to slavery.

36 sc. *Hpæt sæȝst þu.*

ʒea, leof, ic hæbbe : on foreperdne morʒen ic drife sceap
Etiam, habeo : in primo mane mino oues
mine to heora læse, 7 stande ofer hiʒ on hæte 7 on cyle
meas ad pascua, et sto super eas in estu et frigore
mid hundum, þe læs pulfas forspelʒen hiʒ, 7 ic aʒenlæde
cum canibus, ne lupi deuorent eas, et reduco
hiʒ on heora loca, 7 melke hiʒ tpeopa on dæʒ, 7 heora   40
eas ad caulas, et mulgeo eas bis in die, et caulas
loca   ic hæbbe, on þærto 7 cyse 7 buteran ic do ; 7 ic
earum moueo, insuper et caseum et butirum facio ; et
eom ʒetrype hlaforde minon.
fidelis sum domino meo.
Eala, oxanhyrde, hpæt pyrst þu ?
O, bubulce, quid operaris tu ?
Eala, hlaford min, micel ic ʒedeorfe.   Þænne se yrþlinʒc
O, domine mi, multum laboro.   Quando arator
unscenþ þa oxan, ic læde hiʒ to læse, 7 ealle niht ic stande   45
disiungit boues, ego duco eos ad pascua, et tota nocte sto
ofer hiʒ paciende for þeofan, 7 eft on ærnemergen ic betæce
super eos uigilando propter fures, et iterum primo mane adsigno
hiʒ þam yrþlincʒe pel ʒefylde 7 ʒepæterode.
eos aratori bene pastos et adaquatos.

       40 *on* 1] 7   *tpeopa] treopa*   46 *iterum] iteru*

---

38 *mine :* late WSax neut.pl. in *e* (Sievers(Cook) § 293 note 3).
40 *on heora loca :* MS 7 *heora loca,* the scribe evidently misled by
the same words further on.   *loca :* LWS acc.neut.pl. (Sievers(Cook)
§ 237 note 5).   On moving the fold v. H. S. Bennett, *op. cit.* 77f.
For the milking of ewes, *v.* illustration in Luttrell Psalter, fol.
163b. *melke :* cf. Sievers(Cook) § 387 note 3, Luick § 137 Anm. 3.
41 *hæbbe :* glosses *moueo ;* either the scribe has written the 1st
pers.sg.pres. of *habban,* or this is an inverted spelling of *hebbe.*   Cf.
O. Schlutter, *Neophilologus* vii. 214, who quotes a charter of a
Cambridge guild (B. Thorpe, *Diplomatarium Ævi Saxonici* 612),
7 *ʒif hpa fotsetlan hæbbe, do þæt ilce.*   For the above, Schlutter
proposes to read *onhæbbe,* but *on* is above the *in* of *insuper.*   *insuper :* Wright-Wülcker punctuate with the comma after *insuper,*
but the readings of J, R₁, where it follows *butirum,* suggest the
above reading.
45 Cf. Cædmon's duties as a herdsman (Bede, *Hist. Eccles.* IV. 24).
For an example of cattle thieving, so common in Saxon times, v.
a charter printed by F. E. Harmer, *English Historical Documents* 32.

Ys þæs of þinum ȝeferum ?
Est iste ex tuis sociis ?

Ʒea, he ys.
Etiam est.

Canst þu æniȝ þinȝ ?   50
Scis tu aliquid ?

Ænne cræft ic cann.
Unam artem scio.

Hpylcne ?
Qualem ?

Hunta ic eom.
Uenator sum.

Hpæs ?
Cuius ?

Cincȝes.   55
Regis.

Hu beȝæst þu cræft þinne ?
Quomodo exerces artem tuam ?

Ic brede me max 7 sette hiȝ on stope ȝehæppre, 7 ȝetihte
Plecto mihi retia et pono ea in loco apto, et instigo

hundas mine þæt pildeor hiȝ ehton, oþþæt hiȝ becuman
canes meos ut feras persequantur, usque quo perueniunt

to þam nettan unforsceapodlice 7 þæt hiȝ spa beon
ad retia inprouise et sic

beȝrynodo, 7 ic ofslea hiȝ on þam maxum.   60
inretientur, et ego iugulo eas in retibus.

Ne canst þu huntian buton mid nettum ?
Nescis uenare nisi cum retibus ?

---

[51] *Hpylcne*] hpylcne ys   *Qualem*] quale est   [58] *becuman*] þe cuman
[60] *maxum*] maxð   *eas*] eos

---

[51] *Hpylcne* : MS *hpylcne ys* (quale est).   J has *qualem* only.
Thorpe, without comment, cut out the gloss *ys* and altered *quale*
to *qualis* : this, however, does not correspond to the gloss *hpylcne*,
as the reading of J does.   The original no doubt had *qualð*, which
was misread and copied as *quale*, then *est* (with the accompanying
ys) added to obtain the required meaning (cf. Zupitza, *op. cit.* 38).
[58] *becuman* : MS *þe cuman*. Wyatt, *op. cit.* 219, following
Wright-Wülcker's text, suggests taking *þe* with the preceding
oþþæt. Stevenson suggests *becuman*.

Ʒea, butan nettum huntian ic mæʒ.

Etiam sine retibus uenare possum.

Hu ?

Quomodo ?

Mid spiftum hundum ic betæce pildeor.

Cum uelocibus canibus insequor feras.

Hpilce pildeor spyþost ʒefehst þu ?   65

Quales feras maxime capis ?

Ic ʒefeo heortas 7 baras 7 rann 7 ræʒan 7 hpilon haran.

Capio ceruos et apros et dammas et capreos et aliquando lepores.

Þære þu todæʒ on huntnoþe ?

Fuisti hodie in uenatione ?

Ic næs, forþam sunnandæʒ ys, ac ʒyrstandæʒ ic pæs on

Non fui, quia dominicus dies est, sed heri fui in

huntunʒe.

uenatione.

Hpæt ʒelæhtest þu ?   70

Quid cepisti ?

⁶⁴ betæce] betæcc   ⁶⁵ ʒefehst] ʒefeht   ⁶⁷ huntnoþe] huntnolde

---

⁶² ʒea (etiam) : Zupitza, *op. cit.* 44, points out that *etiam* = 'also', not 'yes'.

⁶⁴ *betæce* : *betæcc* MS. Wyatt, *op. cit.* 219, says this gives no proper sense and probably ought to be *becǣce* (= ME *bikeche(n)* catch, ensnare). *Betǣcan*, however, makes possible sense with the meaning 'show', 'point out' (NED beteach ¹) : the hunter uses the dogs to 'point' the game. BT translates 'pursue', the meaning of the Latin.

⁶⁵ *Hpilce* : cf *mine* ³⁸ for the inflexion : Wright-Wülcker has *hpilcc.*

⁶⁶ *ʒefeo* : so MS, which seems indefensible (cf. *ʒefo* ⁸¹) ; perhaps the scribe began again to write *ʒefehst*, which occurs three words earlier. After *ceruos* occurs, in J, an addition of Bata, the names of numerous other animals ranging from the wolf and bear to the ape and hedgehog : the lists derive from Ælfric's *Glossary* (ed. Zupitza, 309). *Dammas* : cf. Ælfric's *Glossary* (ed. Zupitza, 309), damma uel dammula, *da* ; here the name of the species (roe) is given. *capreos* : all texts read this, although f.pl. *capreas* is needed to agree with *ræʒan,* cf. *Glossary* (ed. Zupitza, 309), caprea *ræʒe.*

⁶⁸ On the strict observance of the Sabbath in Saxon times cf. the Laws (e.g. Wihtred, 9 ff). *ʒyrstandæʒ* : Sievers(Cook) § 179 note.

Tpeʒen heortas 7 ænne bar.

Duos ceruos et unum aprum.

Hu ʒefencʒe þu hiʒ ?

Quomodo cepisti eos ?

Heortas ic ʒefenʒc on nettum 7 bar ic ofsloh.

Ceruos cepi in retibus et aprum iugulaui.

Hu pære þu dyrstiʒ ofstikian bar ?

Quomodo fuisti ausus iugulare aprum ?

Hundas bedrifon hyne to me, 7 ic þær toʒeanes standende   75

   Canes perduxerunt eum ad me, et ego econtra stans

færlice ofstikode hyne.

subito iugulaui eum.

Spyþe þryste þu pære þa.

Ualde audax fuisti tunc.

Ne sceal hunta forhtfull pesan, forþam mislice pildeor

   Non debet uenator formidolosus esse, quia uarie bestie

puniað on pudum.

morantur in siluis.

Hpæt dest þu be þinre huntunʒe ?   80

   Quid facis de tua uenatione ?

Ic sylle cynce spa hpæt spa ic ʒefo, forþam ic eom

      Ego do regi quicquid capio, quia sum

hunta hys.

uenator eius.

Hpæt sylþ he þe ?

   Quid dat ipse tibi ?

He scryt me pel 7 fett 7 hpilon sylþ me hors oþþe beah,

Uestit me bene et pascit, aliquando dat mihi equum aut armillam,

⁷³ ʒefenʒc] ʒefcnʒc	⁷⁶ standende] stantende
⁸¹ cynce] cync	⁸⁴ aut armillam] autar millam

---

⁷³ ʒefenʒc : so MS : Wright-Wülcker read ʒefenʒe, which Wyatt, *op. cit.* 219, changes to ʒefenʒ, explaining that it cannot be past subjunctive.

⁷⁵ bedrifon : Stevenson reads bedrufon.

⁷⁹ Here follows in J, in answer to the question *Et quae ?*, a long list of animals which inhabit the woods : it derives mainly from the *Glossary* (ed. Zupitza, 308–10).

⁸³ The addition in J is interesting : *Uel cuius honoris es inter tuos socios ? Primum locum teneo in sua aula. Uestitum autem et*

þæt þe lustlicor cræft minne ic beȝancȝe.   85
ut libentius artem meam exerceam.

Hpylcne cræft canst þu?
Qualem artem scis tu?

Ic eom fiscere.
Ego sum piscator.

Hpæt beȝyst þu of þinum cræfte?
Quid adquiris de tua arte?

Biȝleofan 7 scrud 7 feoh.
Uictum et uestitum et pecuniam.

Hu ȝefehst þu fixas?   90
Quomodo capis pisces?

Ic astiȝie min scyp 7 pyrpe max mine on ea, 7 ancȝil
Ascendo nauem et pono retia mea in amne, et hamum
vel æs ic pyrpe 7 spyrtan, 7 spa hpæt spa hiȝ ȝehæftað ic
proicio et sportas, et quicquid ceperint
ȝenime.
sumo.

Hpæt ȝif hit unclæne beoþ fixas?
Quid si inmundi fuerint pisces?

| 85 *lustlicor*] *lusticor* | 98 *spyrtan*] *spyrtan* |
| 94 *beoþ*] *beoþ beoþ* | *inmundi*] *in mundo* |

---

uictum satis mihi tribuit, et aliquando uero anulum mihi aureum
reddit, et uestit . . . Schröder, *op. cit.* 288, pointing out the derange-
ment of question and answer, suggests the *venator regis* as a possible
parallel (cf. H. Brunner, *Deutsche Rechtsgeschichte* (1928) II. 141),
although his position was rather that of an inferior official. For
gifts to the *venatores regis* (of money, horses), cf L. M. Larson, *The
King's Household in England before the Norman Conquest* (Madison,
Wisconsin 1904) 175 note 62.

91 *astiȝie* : Wyatt, *op. cit.*, emends to *astiȝe* (cf. 153), but it is
possible that we have here the weak *astiȝian*. *æs* : ' the glossator
appears to have been doubtful of the meaning of *hamus* ; the word
æs means bait ' (Wright-Wülcker). Zupitza, *op. cit.* 44, however,
defends the glossator, pointing out that *hamus* was often used with
the sense ' bait '.

94 *Hpæt . . . fixas* : the MS repeats *beoþ*, but the construction
is still awkward. At the end of one line is Quid si in mundo (*hpæt
ȝif hit unclæne beoþ*), the next line begins fuerint pisces (*beoþ fixas*).
It is difficult to explain the presence of *hit*, which was in the original
because the scribe has had to alter its first letter from *u*, as if he

Ic utpyrpe þa unclænan ut, 7 ȝenime me clæne to mete. 95
Ego proiciam inmundos foras, et sumo mihi mundos in escam.

Hpær cypst þu fixas þine?
Ubi uendis pisces tuos?

On ceastre.
In ciuitate.

Hpa biȝþ hi?
Quis emit illos?

Ceasterpara. Ic ne mæȝ spa fela spa ic mæȝ ȝesyllan.
Ciues. Non possum tot capere quot possum uendere.

Hpilce fixas ȝefehst þu? 100
Quales pisces capis?

Ælas 7 hacodas, mynas 7 æleputan, sceotan 7 lampredan,
Anguillas et lucios, menas et capitones, tructas et murenas,

95 *unclænan*] *ut clænan   inmundos*] *in mundo   foras*] deleted by
four dots underneath.

99 *fela*] *fela spa ic mæȝ spa fela*   **101** *tructas*] *tructos*

had at first omitted it and gone on to write *unclæne*. Possibly
the OE read originally *hpæt ȝif hit unclæne beo*, referring back to
spa hpæt spa: the presence of *fuerint pisces* in the next line led
subsequently to the addition of *beoþ fixas* and the alteration of *beo*
to *beoþ*. *inmundi*, *inmundos* are the readings of J. Stevenson
says in error, that *beoþ beoþ* occurs in J. Cf. Deut. xiv. 10 ' what-
soever hath not fins and scales ' is unclean fish according to Mosaic
Law.

95 *foras :* four dots underneath denote that it is to be deleted.

99 The careless gloss suggests that the scribe was copying
mechanically. After *fela* sc. *ȝefon.*

101 *menas et capitones* (mynas 7 æleputan) : ' Minnow probably
represents OE *mynpe*, wk.fem. glossing L. *capedo*, i.e. *capito*, a
fish with a large head. The recorded OE *myne* sb.masc. (pl. *mynas*)
glosses L. *capito* and *mena* : it is not certain what fish was meant.
The L. *capito* is also rendered *æleputa* EELPOUT (NED sub MINNOW).
Cf Wright-Wülcker 180, *capito*, myne uel ælepute : on the development *myne-minnow*, cf. A. S.Napier, *Modern Language Quarterly* i. 52.
tructas (sceotan) : the usual gloss is *truht* (cf. *Glossary*, ed. Zupitza,
308). For *sceota* cf. Gnomic Verses 39, *leax sceal on pæle mid sceote
scriðan*, and R. Carew, *Cornwall* (London 1602) I. 26, ' the Shote
is in maner peculiar to Deuon and Cornwall, in shape and colour
he resembleth the Trowt : howbeit in bignesse and goodnesse,
commeth farre behind him '. *murenas* (lampredan) : Prof. P.
Barbier draws my attention to the fact that the muraena is not
a lamprey.

27

7 spa pylce spa on pætere spymmaþ. Sprote.

et qualescumque in amne natant. Saliu.

Forhþi ne fixast þu on sæ ?

Cur non piscaris in mari ?

Hþilon ic do, ac seldon, forþam micel repyt me ys to sæ.

Aliquando facio, sed raro, quia magnum nauigium mihi est ad mare.

Hþæt fehst þu on sæ ?

Quid capis in mari ?

105

---

[103] *Saliu* (sprote) : Not in J, R$_1$. Thorpe, *Analecta Anglo-Saxonica* (1834) 106 note, reads *salu*, adding ' what is intended by *sprote*, as well as by *salu*, I am at a loss to conjecture '. In the edition of 1846 (23), ' I am unable to explain *salu* otherwise than by supposing it may be an error for *salice* '. Zupitza, *op. cit.* 38, is evidently correct in supposing that the word and its gloss had been added in the margin of an earlier version of C, and incorporated into the body of the text by a later scribe. If this be so, the fact that the fish is included in the freshwater group has no significance. It is noteworthy that *Saliu* is bounded by stops and has a capital *S*. Zupitza, *op. cit.* 38, suggests that the word is a corruption of *salmo*, which however hardly answers to ' sprat '. J. J. Köhler, *Die altenglischen Fischnamen* 79, has no suggestion to offer, but O. Schlutter, in a review of his book (ESt xl. 242) is of the opinion that *saliu* is not the lemma for *sprote*, but an OE word, a mis-reading or variant of *scliu = sliu (sliw)* m. ' tench ', ' mullet ' (cf. Wright-Wülcker, *op. cit.* 180, tinca, *sliw* : cf. 261, 293). A. S. Napier, *Old English Lexicography*, s.v. *culling*, quotes from MS 17 in St. John's College, Oxford, the gloss *silurus*, sprot ; perhaps *saliu* is a corruption of this ? Yet it is very probable that the two words had originally nothing to do with each other, but became associated by being written near each other in the margin. If this is so, then we might guess *saliu* to be a mistake for some form of *salum*, ' open sea ', or of *sal*, ' salt sea ', and that the word was originally put in the margin to distinguish between the two lists of fish. Professor Paul Barbier of Leeds University in a letter writes : ' If *sprote* is *really* glossed by the word spelt *saliu*, I should be inclined to think it might be some derivation of *sal*, applied to a salted clupeid.' Elsewhere *sprott* occurs only in Byrhtferth's *Manual* (ed. S. J. Craw-ford (EETS), 82 *þa lytlan sprottas*, and in Ælfric's *Homilies* (ed. W. W. Skeat) 31, 1271. Köhler, *op. cit.*, assumes the form *sprote* to be a f. by-form of *sprot(t)*, here probably in the plural.

[104] An example of the Anglo-Saxon's apparent dislike of perilous expeditions into the open sea. The prominence given to Ohthere's whale-hunting in Ælfred's *Orosius* also suggests that this occupation was not often followed in Saxon times.

Hæringʒas 7 leaxas, merespyn 7 ştirian, ostran 7 crabban,
Alleces et isicios, delfinos et sturias, ostreas et cancros,

muslan, pinepinclan, sæcoccas, faʒc 7 floc 7 lopystran
musculas, torniculi, neptigalli, platesia et platissa et polipodes

7 fela spylces.
et similia.

Þylt þu fon sumne hpæl ?
Uis capere aliquem cetum ?

Nic.   110
Nolo.

Forhᵖi ?
Quare ?

Forþam plyhtlic þinʒc hit ys ʒefon hpæl.   Ʒebeorhlicre
Quia periculosa res est capere cetum.   Tutius

---

¹⁰⁷ *faʒc*] altered from *facc*   ¹¹² *Forþam*] *forhpan*   *plyhtlic*] *pbyhtlic*
þinʒc]*þnʒč*   *ʒebeorhlicre*]*ʒebeorhtlicre*   *tutius*] *tutuis*

---

¹⁰⁶ ' Herrings come first because they were more extensively used than any other kind of fish ' (Wright-Wülcker).

¹⁰⁷ Zupitza, *op. cit.* 38, points out that in J *et polipodes* follows immediately after *musculas* (before which *mugiles et fannos, roceas* is interpolated) and that the four extra names (found only in C) *torniculi . . . platissa* are in the nom. case, and the last two in the singular : cf. Schröder, *op. cit.* 284.   *pinepinclan :* cf. C. H. Whiteman, *Anglia* xxx. 381.   *faʒc :* so Thorpe and Flom, but most editors read *faʒe*, although the MS clearly has *faʒc*. ʒ has been written over a *c*, but the rising hair-line of the foot still shows and gives to the last letter of the word the appearance of *e*.   *facʒ* occurs in the vocabulary printed by Wright-Wülcker, *op. cit.* 180 : platesia, *facʒ*.   Köhler, *op. cit.* 31, tries to defend the form *faʒe*, but Schlutter, ESt xl. 238, prefers *facʒ* (*faʒc*), which he thinks a re-reading of the MS will establish, drawing attention to the variation *cʒ, ʒc* in Ælfric.   For the etymology, he compares NE dial. *fadge* ' a large flat loaf or bannock ' ; the *platesia* is the flat fish.   F. Holthausen, *Altenglisches etymologisches Wörterbuch*, also gives this suggestion with a query, and suggests *faʒe* as an acc.pl., whereas we need a sg. form here.   *lopystran :* v. J. d. Z. Cortelyou, *Anglistische Forschungen* xix. 119.

¹¹² *ʒebeorhlicre :*   MS *ʒebeorhtlicre*, by confusion between *beorh* and *beorht.*

ys me faran to ea mid scype mynan, þænne faran mid
est mihi ire ad amnem cum hamo meo, quam ire cum
maneȝum scypum on huntunȝe hranes.
multis nauibus in uenationem ballene.

Forhpi spa ?   115
Cur sic ?

Forþam leofre ys me ȝefon fisc þæne ic mæȝ ofslean,
Quia carius est mihi capere piscem quem possum occidere,
þonne fisc, þe na þæt an me ac eac spylce mine ȝeferan
quam illum, qui non solum me sed etiam meos socios
mid anum sleȝe he mæȝ besencean oþþe ȝecpylman.
uno ictu potest mergere aut mortificare.

7 þeah mæniȝe ȝefoþ hpælas, 7 ætberstaþ frecnysse,
Et tamen multi capiunt cetos, et euadunt pericula,

7 micelne sceat þanon beȝytaþ.   120
et magnum pretium inde adquirunt.

Soþ þu seȝst, ac ic ne ȝeþristȝe for modes mines
Uerum dicis, sed ego non audeo propter mentis meę
nytenyssæ.
ignauiam.

Hpæt sæȝst þu, fuȝelere ?   Hu bespicst þu fuȝelas ?
Quid dicis tu, auceps ?   Quomodo decipis aues ?

113 *hamo meo]homo mea*   117 *quam illum*] supplied from J
þonne fisc] not in MS   119 *cetos*] *cecos*   121 *ȝeþristȝe*] altered from
ȝeþriste   123 *auceps*] an indecisive attempt to correct from *aciceps*

---

113 *hamo* (scype) : Wright-Wülcker alter to *naue*, but J has
hamo, which is likely to have been the original, possibly glossed
wrongly because of *scypum* later.

117 *quam illum :* supplied from J, which Zupitza, *op. cit.* 39,
thinks preserves the original here. He also answers Wright's objec-
tion (Wright-Wülcker, *op. cit.*, Original Introd. vii. note) that *solum*
is ' translated as an adj., instead of an adverb ', by quoting from
Ælfric's *Homilies* II. 468 : *he hine ȝeseah na þæt an mid lichamlicere
ȝesihðe ac eac spilce . . .; he :* an attempt to provide a subject
for *mæȝ*.

121 *ȝeþristȝe : ȝ* written over a previous *i :* cf. Sievers(Cook) § 412
note 1.

122 *nytenyssæ :* cf. Bülbring § 571 (cf. *forlidenesse* 156).

123 Zupitza, *op. cit.* 40, points out that on the analogy of previous
questions we should expect ' What birds do you catch ? ' and
suggests a gap here in C. In J, Bata has added, after *auceps,*

On feala pisan ic bespice fuʒelas : hpilon mid neton,
Multis modis decipio aues : aliquando retibus,

    mid ʒrinum,   mid lime,   mit [125]
    aliquando laqueis, aliquando glutino, aliquando

hpistlunʒe,   mid hafoce,   mid treppan.
    sibilo, aliquando accipitre, aliquando decipula.

Hæfst þu hafoc ?
Habes accipitrem ?

Ic hæbbe.
Habeo.

Canst þu temian hiʒ ?
Scis domitare eos ?

Ʒea, ic cann. Hpæt sceoldon hiʒ me buton ic cuþe [130]
    Etiam, scio. Quid deberent mihi nisi scirem

temian hiʒ ?
domitare eos ?

Syle me ænne hafoc.
Da mihi unum accipitrem.

Ic sylle lustlice, ʒyf þu sylst me ænne spiftne hund.
    Dabo libenter, si dederis mihi unum uelocem canem.

Hpilcne hafoc pilt þu habban, þone maran hpæþer þe
    Qualem accipitrem uis habere, maiorem aut

[124] *bespice*] þespice   [124] *hafoc*] hafac

Quales aues sepissime capis ? and, in reply, a long list of bird-names (cf. *Glossary*, ed. Zupitza, 307–8). Schröder, *op. cit.* 287, denies any omission and argues, rightly, that variety is being aimed at by Ælfric, who ' mit einer verächtlichen kopfwendung halbrück-wärts ' passes on to the next pupil, asking not what birds he catches but how he does it. Notice also his ingenuity in contrasting the timidity of the fisherman with the daring of the hunter.

[124] *pisan :* late WSax for *pisena* (Sievers(Cook) § 276 note 4), or adject. use of *feala. feala :* cf. Schlemilch 34 Anm. 1.

[126] For hawking in Anglo-Saxon days, cf. Hoops *Reallex* II. 7–9, M. Ashdown, *English and Norse Documents* (Cambridge 1930) 73 ; for representations, cf. Hoops *Reallex* I. 26, Brit. Mus. MS Jul. A vi. and Luttrell Psalter fol. 163 (for bird-snaring fol. 18).

[130] *sceoldon :* sc. *fremian.*

[131] Although there is no MS warrant for the suggestion (not even in R₁), it is possible, as supposed by Wright-Wülcker, that this is spoken by the hunter.

[134] The normal order would be *hpæþer þone maran þe þæne* . . .

þæne læssan ?

minorem ?

Syle me þæne maran.

Da mihi maiorem.

Hu afest þu hafocas þine ?

Quomodo pascis accipitres tuos ?

Hiȝ fedaþ hiȝ sylfe 7 me on pintra, 7 on lencȝten ic

Ipsi pascunt se et me in hieme, et in uere

læte hiȝ ætpindan to puda, 7 ȝenyme me briddas on

dimitto eos auolare ad siluam, et capio mihi pullos in

hærfæste, 7 temiȝe hiȝ.   140

autumno, et domito eos.

7 forhpi forlæst þu þa ȝetemedon ætpindan fram þe ?

Et cur permittis domitos auolare a te ?

Forþam ic nelle fedan hiȝ on sumera, forþamþe hiȝ

Quia nolo pascere eos in estate, eo quod

þearle etaþ.

nimium comedunt.

7 maniȝe fedaþ þa ȝetemodon ofer sumor, þæt eft hiȝ

Et multi pascunt domitos super estatem, ut iterum

habban ȝearupe.   145

habeant paratos.

Ȝea, spa hiȝ doþ, ac ic nelle o þæt an deorfan ofer hiȝ,

Etiam, sic faciunt, sed ego nolo in tantum laborare super eos,

forþam ic cann oþre, na þæt ænne, ac eac spilce maniȝe

quia scio alios, non solum unum, sed etiam plures

ȝefon.

capere.

¹³⁹ *pullos*] *pullo*   ¹⁴⁸ *capere*] *cape*

---

¹³⁹ Cf. *Maldon* 7–8, *Offan mæȝ* had no further use for his hawk.
¹⁴³ Cf. ' as hungry as a hawk '.
¹⁴⁴ *hiȝ habban :* subject *hiȝ,* object *ȝearupe* (sc. *hafocas*).   *habban :*
pres.subj. (Sievers(Cook) § 416 note 1c).
¹⁴⁶ *o þæt an :* mechanical glossing, an attempt to render *in
tantum* (so greatly).   Of the two meanings of *tantum* (so much,
only) *þæt an* gives the wrong one here.   A. J. Wyatt, *The Threshold
of Anglo-Saxon* 7, reads *spa micel.*
¹⁴⁷ Here, influenced by the Latin and the following *ænne,* the
usual *an* is omitted between *þæt* and *ænne.*

Hpæt sæȝst þu, mancȝere ?
Quid dicis tu, mercator ?

Ic secȝe þæt behefe ic eom ȝe cinȝce 7 eoldormannum [150]
Ego dico quod utilis sum et regi et ducibus

7 peliȝum 7 eallum follce.
et diuitibus et omni populo.

7 hu ?
Et quomodo ?

Ic astiȝe min scyp mid hlæstum minum, 7 rope ofer sælice
Ego ascendo nauem cum mercibus meis, et nauigo ultra marinas

dælas, 7 cype mine þinȝc, 7 bicȝe þincȝ dyrpyrðe þa on
partes, et uendo meas res et emo res pretiosas, quę in

þisum lande ne beoþ acennede, 7 ic hit toȝelæde eop [155]
hac terra non nascuntur, et adduco uobis

hider mid micclan plihte ofer sæ, 7 hpylon forlidenesse ic
huc cum magno periculo super mare, et aliquando naufragium

þolie mid lyre ealra þinȝa minra, uneaþe cpic ætberstende.
patior cum iactura omnium rerum mearum, uix uiuus euadens.

Hpylce þinc ȝelædst þu us ?
Quales res adducis nobis ?

Pællas 7 sidan, deorpyrþe ȝymmas 7 ȝold, selcuþe reaf
Purpuram et sericum, pretiosas gemmas et aurum, uarias uestes

7 pyrtȝemanȝc, pin 7 ele, ylpesban 7 mæstlinȝc, ær 7 tin, [160]
et pigmenta, uinum et oleum, ebur et auricalcum, ęs et stagnum,

[150] *cinȝce*] *cinȝc*   [158] *adducis*] *adduces*   [159] *purpuram*] *purpurum*

---

[149] In Bata's *Colloquia Difficiliora* (Stevenson, 70) one of the class is addressed *O transmarine monache ! de quo monasterio aduenisti tu huc ?* If there was any novice from abroad in Ælfric's class, he would surely be cast for this part.

[150] *cinȝce :* Stevenson *cinȝe.* The MS *cinȝc* has been scratched, and it is difficult to say if there is another letter after -*ȝc :* the word *ȝe* is added above the line of the gloss, the descender of the *ȝ* coming down between *eom* and *cinȝc.*

[156-7] Glosses in J : *forlyðenisse, þolode, ·lire, cucu, ætbirstinde.*

[159] Cf. the Laws (iv. Ethelred) for details of trade regulations and articles of trade (ed. A. J. Robertson, *The Laws of the Kings of England* 70 ff, and notes thereto) ; ' *selcuþe* is not a good rendering of *uarias* ; *faȝe* would be nearer, or perhaps *tpihipe* ' (Dickins).

[160] *ylpesban :* cf. Ælfric, *Lives of the Saints* (ed. W. W. Skeat III. 104), *ylpas ne comon næfre on Engla lande,* followed by a descrip-

spefel 7 ȝlæs, 7 þylces fela.
sulfur et uitrum et his similia.

Þilt þu syllan þinȝc þine her eal spa þu hi ȝebohtest þær ?
Uis uendere res tuas hic sicut emisti illic ?

Ic nelle. Hpæt þænne me fremode ȝedeorf min ? Ac
Nolo. Quid tunc mihi proficit labor meus ? Sed

ic pille heora cypen her luflicor þonne ȝebicȝe þær, þæt
uolo uendere hic carius quam emi illic, ut

sum ȝestreon me ic beȝyte, þanon ic me afede 7 min pif [165]
aliquod lucrum mihi adquiram, unde me pascam et uxorem

7 minne sunu.
et filios.

Þu, sceopyrhta, hpæt pyrcst þu us nytpyrþnessæ ?
Tu, sutor, quid operaris nobis utilitatis ?

Ys, pitodlice, cræft min behefe þearle eop 7 neodþearf.
Est quidem ars mea utilis ualde uobis et necessaria.

Hu ?
Quomodo ?

Ic bicȝe hyda 7 fell, 7 ȝearkie hiȝ mid cræfte minon, [170]
Ego emo cutes et pelles, et preparo eas arte mea,

[161] *uitrum*] *utrum*   [164] *pille*] *pielle*   [167] *quid*] *d* added
above the line, with caret under

---

tion of an elephant. *mæstlinȝc :* cf. Sievers(Cook) § 196 note 4 (cf.
mistlices 171, *mislice* 78).

[162] According to the code *Be leod-ȝeþincðum* (ed. F. Liebermann
I. 456), the merchant who has crossed the seas three times at his
own expense is entitled to *ȝesiðcund* status.

[163] *fremode :* subj. J has the gloss *fremað*. *pille :* MS *pielle*,
the scribe first wrote *ic nelle*, influenced by the same words just
before : then *p* was written over *n*, covering only the first down-
stroke.

[164] *luflicor :* ' lit. " more lovingly ", a literal translation of the
Latin *carius* in one of its meanings and that the wrong one . . .
it is extraordinary that the translator did not use the comp.adv.
dieror ' (A. J. Wyatt, *op. cit.* 220). He also says that such a mistake could not be Ælfric's work. A. S. Cook, *First Book in Old
English* 131, suggests that the original might have been *lēoflicor*.
Cf. Zupitza, *op. cit.* 44.

[165] *beȝyte, afede :* pres.subj.

[166] *minne sunu :* the Latin has the plural.

7 pyrce of him ʒescy mistlices cynnes, spyftleras 7 sceos,
et facio ex eis calciamenta diuersi generis, subtalares et ficones,
leþerhosa 7 butericas, bridelþpancʒas 7 ʒeræda, flaxan
caligas et utres, frenos et falera, flascones
vel pinnan 7 hiʒdifatu, spurleþera 7 hælftra, pusan 7
et casidilia, calcaria et chamos, peras et
fætelsas ; 7 nan eoper nele oferpintran buton minon cræfte.
marsupia ; et nemo uestrum uult hiemare sine mea arte.
sealtera, hpæt us fremaþ cræft þin ?   **175**
O salinator, quid nobis proficit ars tua ?
þearle fremaþ cræft min eop eallum.   Nan eoper blisse
Multum prodest ars mea omnibus.   Nemo uestrum gaudio
brycð on ʒererduncʒe oþþe mete, buton cræft min ʒistliþe
fruitur in prandio aut cena, nisi ars mea hospita
him beo.
ei fuerit.
Hu ?
Quomodo ?
Hpylc manna þurhperodum þurhbrycþ mettum buton **180**
Quis hominum dulcibus perfruitur cibis sine
spæcce sealtes ?   Hpa ʒefylþ cleafan his oþþe hedderna
sapore salis ?   Quis replet cellaria sua siue promptuaria
buton cræfte minon ?   Efne, buterʒeþpeor ælc 7 cysʒerunn
sine arte mea ?   Ecce, butirum omne et caseum

[171] *caligas*] *coligas*   [173] *spurleþera*] *spurleþera*   [175] *cræft*] *cræfst*
[181] *replet*] *repplet*   [183] *cræfte*] *scræfte*   *arte*] *arce*

---

[172] *leþerhosa :*   Sievers(Cook) § 278 note 1.   Here, apparently,
the word declines like a short ō-stem.
[175] sc. *eala.*   ' Till root crops were introduced, it was difficult,
from lack of fodder, to keep a large herd of cattle all through
the winter ; and accordingly the meat for the winter was ordinarily
prepared and salted down in the autumn ' (Cunningham, *op. cit.*
73).   Cf. the significance of the name *blotmonað* for November,
the Scandinavian practice of killing cattle at *vetrnætr* (' winter-
nights '), and the term *mart* for cattle fattened for slaughter and
killed about Martinmas.
[183] *buterʒeþpeor ælc 7 cysʒerunn .*   Elsewhere in the *Colloquy* (288)
and in the glosses *butirum, caseum* are glossed by *butere, cyse.*   Here
the salter, to emphasize the importance of his craft, uses the words

losaþ eop buton ic hyrde ætpese eop, þe ne furþon þæt an
perit uobis nisi ego custos adsim, qui nec saltem
pyrtum eoprum butan me brucaþ.
oleribus uestris sine me utimini.

               bæcere, hpam fremaþ   oþþe hpæþer [185]
    Quid dicis tu, pistor? Cui prodest ars tua, aut si
þe butan þe maʒon lif adreoʒan ?
  sine te possimus uitam ducere ?

ʒe maʒon   þurh sum fæc butan
Potestis quidem per aliquod spatium sine arte mea uitam

   na lancʒe ne to pel : soþlice butan cræfte minon ælc
ducere, sed non diu nec adeo bene : nam sine arte mea omnis
beod æmtiʒ byþ ʒesepen, 7 buton hlafe ælc mete to plættan
mensa uacua uidetur esse, et sine pane omnis cibus in nausiam
byþ ʒehpyrfed. Ic heortan mannes ʒestranʒie, ic mæʒen [190]
    conuertitur. Ego cor hominis confirmo, ego robur

---

[183] *furþon*] *furþoon*   [185] *pistor*] *pastor*   [189] *pane*] *pané*
nausiam] *nausium*

---

which describe the butter and cheese in an unfinished state : without salt these substances will not keep. BT translates *cysʒerunn*
as ' rennet or runnet, a substance used to produce curd ', but as
O. Schlutter, *Anglia* ci. 158, shows, the word must refer to the
curd itself. He cites Wright-Wülcker 128, coagulatus, *ʒerunnen*,
and the phrase *ʒenim cu meoluc butan pætere læt peorþan to fletum*
ʒeþþer to buteran (Leechdoms II. 108). Thorpe and Stevenson
emend *caseum* to *caseus*, but this related neut. form is used in the
Glossary (ed. Zupitza, 315), and all texts of the *Colloquy* read
caseum.

[183] *þe ne furþon þæt an :* in the MS *þe ne furþoon* [sic] is crowded
over *qui nec* with the abbreviation *þ̄* underneath (and over *nec*) ;
over *saltem* stands *an*. This is either an awkward combination of
the two expressions *ne furþon* and *na þæt an* to render *nec saltem*,
or else *þ̄ an* was added later in an attempt to render *saltem* which
stood apparently unglossed.

[184] *utimini :* R₁ ends here.

[185] sc. *Hpæt sæʒst þu; cræft þin.* From this point onwards
omissions of introductory phrases (e.g. *hpæt sæʒest þu . . .*) are
common in C. *oþþe hpæþer :* ' the direct question *hpam fremaþ* is
irregularly followed by an indirect question and *oþþe* is redundant '
(Wyatt, *The Threshold of Anglo-Saxon* 69).

[187] sc. *cræfte minon lif adreoʒan, ac.*

[189] *byþ ʒesepen :* ' seems ', in imitation of *uidetur.*

pera   7 furþon litlincȝas nellaþ forbiȝean me.
uirorum sum et nec paruuli uolunt preterire me.

                 hpæþer   pe   beþurfon   on   æniȝon
        Quid dicimus de coco, si indigemus in aliquo
cræfte
arte eius?

           ȝif ȝe me ut adrifaþ fram eoprum ȝeferscype,
      Dicit cocus : Si me expellitis a uestro collegio,
ȝe etaþ pyrta eopre ȝrene, 7 flæscmettas eopre hreape, 195
manducabitis holera uestra uiridia, et carnes uestras crudas,

7   furþon fætt broþ ȝe maȝon
et nec saltem pingue ius potestis sine arte mea habere.

Þe ne reccaþ   ne he us neodþearf ys, forþam
   Non curamus de arte tua, nec nobis necessaria est, quia
pe sylfe maȝon seoþan þa þinȝc þe to seoþenne synd, 7
    nos ipsi possumus coquere quę coquenda sunt, et
brædan þa þinȝc þe to brædene synd.
     assare que assanda sunt.

          ȝif ȝe forþy me fram adryfaþ, þæt ȝe þus 200
      Dicit cocus : Si ideo me expellitis, ut sic
don, þonne beo ȝe ealle þrælas, 7 nan eoper ne biþ hlaford ;
faciatis, tunc eritis omnes coci, et nullus uestrum erit dominus ;

195 *uiridia]* uirida   197 *necessaria]* nec cessaria   200 *si ideo]* sudeo

---

191 sc. *eom*   192 sc. *Hpæt secȝe pe be coce.*

193 After *cræfte* sc. *his* (gen. after *beþurfon*) (so Wyatt, *The Threshold of Anglo-Saxon* 69).

194 sc. *Se coc secȝð.* The Latin has here for the first time a direction *dicit cocus ;* in J *econtra dicit cocus.* Cf. also 200, where in J the direction is still more precise, *adhuc dicit cocus et loquitur audacter.*

196 sc. *ne ; butan cræfte minon habban. furþon :* there is no attempt to gloss *nec.*

197 sc. *be cræfte þinon. necessaria :* MS *nec cessaria,* probably influenced by preceding *nec.*

199 *brædene :* cf. Sievers(Cook) § 363 note 2 (cf. *seoþenne* 198).

200 sc. *Se coc secȝð.*

201 *þrælas* is used to gloss *coci* (which occurs in all Latin texts) because it gives an obvious antithesis to *hlaford* (dominus). Wright-Wülcker suggest that *coci* stood in error for *serui.* Zupitza, *op. cit.* 40, defends *coci,* pointing out that the cook's argument is that if each has to turn to to cook for himself, when he is gone, they prove conclusively that cookery is indispensable for everybody.

7 þeahhpæþere buton ȝe ne etaþ.

et tamen sine arte mea non manducabitis.

Eala, munuc, þe me tospycst, efne, ic hæbbe afandod

  O, monache, qui mihi locutus es, ecce, probaui

þe habban ȝode ȝeferan 7 þearle neodþearfe ; 7 ic ahsie þa.

 te habere bonos socios et ualde necessarios ; qui sunt illi ?

Ic hæbbe smiþas, isene smiþas, ȝoldsmiþ, seoloforsmiþ, **205**

  Habeo fabros, ferrarios, aurificem, argentarium,

arsmiþ, treoppyrhtan 7 maneȝra oþre mistlicra cræfta

  ęrarium, lignarium et multos alios uariarum artium

biȝȝenceras.

 operatores.

Hæfst æniȝne þisne ȝeþeahtan ?

 Habes aliquem sapientem consiliarium ?

Ȝepislice ic hæbbe. ure ȝeȝaderunȝc buton

  Certe habeo. Quomodo potest nostra congregatio sine

ȝeþeahtynde beon þissod ？   **210**

  consiliario regi ?

[202] *manducabitis*] *manducatis*	[205] *ferrarios*] *ferrarium*
[204] *treoppyrhtan*] *treoppyrtan*	[208] *æniȝne*] *æniȝre*

---

[202] sc. *cræfte minon*. *manducabitis : manducatis* MS. Cf Zupitza, *op. cit.* 41.

[204] *ic ahsie þa* (Qui sunt illi) : J has here . . . *et ualde necessarios. Et interrogo te, si adhuc habes aliquos tales his exceptis.*

Etiam, habeo plures ualde necessarios et optimos.

Qui sunt illi ?

Zupitza, *op. cit.* 41, first drew attention to the fact that *ic ahsie þa* glosses *qui sunt illi* incorrectly, and suggested that the scribe of C had jumped from the first *necessarios* to the second, consequently omitting part of his original, although he went on to begin the gloss of the missing portion. Zupitza thinks J approximately preserves the original here (probably with the omission of *optimos*, although R₂ includes this and omits *necessarios et*). *þa* is either a mistake for *þu* (interrogo *te*) or else the scribe found the right place again and wrote, correctly, *þa* above *illi*.

[205] *ferrarios :* so R₂ which corresponds to the gloss. CJ *ferrarium*.

[206] *maneȝra mistlicra cræfta* depends (in gen.pl.) on (*oþre*) *biȝȝenceras*. Stevenson reads *mistlicre*, but the MS has clearly -*a*.

[209] sc. *Hu mæȝ*

[210] *þissod :* cf. Sievers(Cook) § 230 note 1.

pisa, hpilc cræft þe ʒeþuht betpux þas
Quid dicis tu, sapiens? Que ars tibi uidetur inter istas
furþra pesan ?
prior esse ?

me ys ʒeþuht Ꝼodes þeopdom betpeoh þas
Dico tibi, mihi uidetur seruitium Dei inter istas
cræftas ealdorscype healdan, spa spa hit ʒeræd on
artes primatum tenere, sicut legitur in
ʒodspelle : " Fyrmest secea∂ rice Ꝼodes 7 rihtpisnesse [215]
euangelio : " Primum querite regnum Dei et iustitiam
hys, 7 þas þinʒc ealle beoþ toʒehyhte eop."
eius, et hęc omnia adicientur uobis."

7 hpilc þe ʒeþuht betpux poruldcræftas heoldan
Et qualis tibi uidetur inter artes seculares retinere
ealdordom ?
primatum ?

Eorþtilþ, forþam se yrþlinʒ us ealle fett.
Agricultura, quia arator nos omnes pascit.

Se smiþ secʒ∂ : Hpanon sylan scear oþþe culter, þe na [220]
Ferrarius dicit : Unde aratori uomer aut culter, qui nec
ʒade hæfþ buton of cræfte minon ? Hpanon fiscere ancʒel,
stimulum habet nisi ex arte mea ? Unde piscatori hamus,

[213] *Dei*] added above line, with caret under line   [216] *adicientur*]
adicienter   [217] *poruldcræftas*] *cræftas poruld   Et qualis*] *Etquales*
with *t* added above line   [220] *dicit*] *dici*

---

[211] sc. *Hpæt sæʒst þu :* sc. *ys* to render *uidetur :* cf. *ʒeræd* 214,
ʒeþuht 217.

[213] sc. *Ic secʒe þe*

[217] *poruldcræftas :* MS *cræftas poruld ;* the influence of the Latin
disturbs the usual compound.

[220] *sylan :* plainly the gloss to *aratori.* A. S. Napier, *Old English
Glosses* 63, has stibarius i. arator, syla, sulhandla (Aldhelm, De Laud.
Virg. fol. 39), and the note ' syla (= *sulhjon*) is only recorded
here '. The *Colloquy* provides a second example of the meaning
' ploughman '. Cf. J. R. Clark Hall, *Anglo-Saxon Dictionary*, s.v.
syla, and O. Schlutter, *Neophilologus* vii. 212.   Wright-Wülcker read
(*þam yrþlinʒc*) *sylanscear ;* Cook, *op. cit.* 132, emends to *sulhscear*
and supplies *∂æm ier∂linʒe ;* Wyatt, *The Threshold of Anglo-
Saxon* 8, reads *þæm yrþlinʒe sylan scear*, but does not gloss *sylan.*

oþþe sceopyrhton æl, oþþe seamere nædl ? Nis hit of
aut sutori subula, siue sartori acus? Nonne ex

minon ʒepeorce ?
meo opere ?

Se ʒeþeahtend 7speraþ : Soþ pitodlice sæʒst, ac eallum
Consiliarius respondit : Uerum quidem dicis, sed omnibus

us leofre ys pikian mid þe, yrþlincʒe, þonne mid þe, forþam **225**
nobis carius est hospitari apud te aratorem quam apud te, quia

se yrþlinʒ sylð us hlaf 7 drenc ; þu, hpæt sylst us on
arator dat nobis panem et potum ; tu, quid das nobis in

smiþþan þinre buton isenne fyrspearcan 7 speʒincʒa
officina tua nisi ferreas scintillas et sonitus

beatendra slecʒea 7 blapendra byliʒa ?
tundentium malleorum et flantium follium ?

Se treoppyrhta seʒð : Hpilc eoper ne notaþ cræfte minon,
Lignarius dicit : Quis uestrum non utitur arte mea,

þonne hus 7 mistlice fata 7 scypa eop eallum ic pyrce ? **230**
cum domos et diuersa uasa et naues omnibus fabrico ?

Se ʒolsmiþ 7pyrt : Eala, tryppyrhta, forhpi spa sprycst
Ferrarius respondit : O, lignarie, cur sic loqueris,

---

222 *sartori acus*] *saltoriacus*   **225** *te* ¹] added above line
227 *fyrspearcan*] *fyrpearcan officina*] *officia scintillas*] *scinctillas*
228 *flantium*] *flantiu*   **231** *tryppyrhta*] *tryppyrta   sprycst*] *sprycsi*

---

222 *æl :* cf. O. Schlutter, *Anglia* xl. 352.

224 *sæʒst : þu* is omitted, although there is room for it before *ac.*
Cf. *sylst* 226.

225 *te* inserted above the line, with the gloss *þe* above. J suggests that *apud aratorem* was the original reading (Zupitza, *op. cit.*
39). Cook and Wyatt emend *þe* to *þæm*, but this destroys the
value of the addition : the Consiliarius points to each of the disputants in turn. It is possible, of course, that the addition was
purely mechanical, influenced by the following *apud te (mid þe)*.

227 *isenne :* cf. *isene* **205**. The form with *nn* is either an unusual
assimilated form of *iserne* (pl. of *isern*), or else the correct *isene*
was taken to be a simplified form of *isenne* (Sievers(Cook) § 296
note 3) which was falsely restored to the text. The effective use
of assonance and alliteration in this passage is characteristic of
some of Ælfric's prose.

231 *ʒolsmiþ :* The Latin has *ferrarius*, not *aurifex* (cf. 220). K.
Jost, *Anglia* li. 196, notes a similar freedom of translation in the

þu, þonne ne furþon an þyrl   þu ne miht don?
cum nec saltem unum foramen sine arte mea uales facere?

Se ᵹeþeahtend sæᵹþ : Eala, ᵹeferan 7 ᵹode pyrhtan,
Consiliarius dicit : O, socii et boni operarii,

uton topurpon hpætlicor þas ᵹeflitu, 7 sy sibb 7 ᵹeþpærnyss
dissoluamus citius has contentiones, et sit pax et concordia

betpeoh us, 7 framiᵹe anra ᵹehpylc oþron on cræfte hys, 7 ²³⁵
inter uos, et prosit unusquisque alteri arte sua, et

ᵹeðpærian symble mid þam yrþlinᵹe, þær þe biᵹleofan us 7
conueniamus semper apud aratorem, ubi uictum nobis et

foddor horsum urum habbaþ. 7 þis ᵹeþeaht ic sylle eallum
pabula equis nostris habemus. Et hoc consilium do omnibus

pyrhtum, þæt anra ᵹehpylc cræft his ᵹeornlice beᵹanᵹe,
operariis, ut unusquisque artem suam diligenter exerceat,

forþam se þe cræft his forlæt, he byþ forlæten fram þam
quia qui artem suam dimiserit, ipse dimittatur ab

cræfte. Spa hpæðer þu sy, spa mæsseprest, spa munuc, ²⁴⁰
arte.   Siue sis   sacerdos, siue monachus,

spa ceorl, spa kempa, beᵹa oþþe behpyrf þe sylfne on þisum,
seu laicus, seu miles, exerce temet ipsum in hoc,

---

²³⁴ *concordia*] *i* added above line   ²³⁵ *anra ᵹehpylc*] *urum ᵹehpylcum   cræfte*] *cræfte*, altered from *fræfte*   ²³⁶ *ᵹeðpærian*] *ᵹedpærian   pe*] *pe*, altered from *po   biᵹleofan*]*bicleofan   us*] *us*, altered from *as*   ²⁴⁰ *cræfte*] written in margin, with *te* and part of *f* covered by mounting of leaf *mæsseprest*] *mæsseprest*, altered from *mæssepfest*   ²⁴¹ *ipsum*] *ipsue*, *e* written over an original *t* (?)

Pentateuch (Gen. iv. 22), where *faber in cuncta opera aeris et ferri* is rendered *se wæs æᵹðer ᵹe ᵹoldsmið ᵹe irensmið.*

²³² sc. *butan cræfte minon*

²³⁵ *anra ᵹehpylc :* MS *urum ᵹehpylcum* ; the correct expression occurs in ²³⁸. Several mistakes and badly formed letters occur in the MS here and in the following lines.

²³⁸ For the sentiment, cf. *ᵹif ðu hpylcne cræft cunne, beᵹa þone ᵹeorne* (J. M. Kemble, *The Dialogue of Salomon and Saturnus* (1848) 266), which A. J. Wyatt, *Anglo-Saxon Reader* 222, suggests is a reminiscence of Cato, *Disticha* iv. 21.

²⁴¹ *beᵹa oþþe behpyrf :* for the first time the glossator follows a frequent practice of OE translators (e.g. the OE version of Bede's *Hist. Eccles.*), and renders the Latin by two words of similar meaning.

41

7 beo þæt þu eart ; forþam micel hynð 7 sceamu hyt is
et esto quod es; quia magnum dampnum et uerecundia est

menn nellan pesan þæt þæt he ys 7 þæt þe he pesan sceal.
homini nolle esse quod est et quod esse debet.

Eala, cild, hu eop licaþ þeos spæc?
O, pueri, quomodo uobis placet ista locutio?

Þel   heo licaþ us, ac þearle deoplice sprycst 7 ofer [245]
Bene quidem placet nobis, sed ualde profunde loqueris et ultra

mæþe ure þu forþtyhst spræce : ac sprec us æfter urum
etatem nostram protrahis sermonem : sed loquere nobis iuxta nostrum

andʒyte, þæt þe maʒon understandan þa þinʒ þe
intellectum, ut possimus intelligere que

þu specst.
loqueris.

Ic ahsiʒe eop, forhpi spa ʒeornlice leorni ʒe?
Interrogo uos cur tam diligenter discitis?

Forþam þe nellaþ pesan spa stunte nytenu, þa nan þinʒ [250]
Quia nolumus esse sicut bruta animalia, quę nihil

pitaþ, buton ʒærs 7 pæter.
sciunt, nisi herbam et aquam.

7 hpæt pille ʒe?
Et quid uultis uos?

---

[242] *hynð*] hynd   [243] *nellan*] nelle   nolle] nelle   [245] *ualde*] l
added above line, with caret beneath   *profunde*] profunde, altered
from profundo   [246] *forþtyhst*] forþtyht   [249] *leorni ʒe*] leornincʒe,
c added above line   *discitis*] deiscitis   [250] *þa*] ba   [251] *ʒærs*] ʒærd

---

[243] *nellan* : MS *nelle*, obviously influenced by *nelle* of the Latin,
which should, however, be *nolle*.

[244] *spæc* : for the lost *r*, cf. *specst* [246] (Sievers(Cook) § 180), yet
cf. *prættiʒe* [254].

[249] *leorni ʒe* : MS *leornincʒe* (*c* written above and between *nʒ*) :
from the Latin we expect the vb. and not the noun : possibly
a form like *leorni ʒe* (Sievers(Cook) § 360 note 3) stood in the
original and was copied as *leorninʒe* in mistake : *c* above the line
may be a later addition.   Wright-Wülcker read *leornia ʒe* without
comment : Stevenson *leornincʒe* [sic].

[250] *þa* : MS *ba*. Stevenson has *þa* [sic] by a misprint.

Þyllaþ pesan pise.
Uolumus esse sapientes.

On hƿilcon pisdome ? Þille ȝe beon prættiȝe oþþe
Qua sapientia ? Uultis esse uersipelles aut

þusenthipe on leasunȝum, lytiȝe on spræcum, onȝlæplice, 255
milleformes in mendaciis, astuti in loquelis, astuti,

hinderȝepe, pel sprecende 7 yfele þencende, spæsum pordum
uersuti, bene loquentes et male cogitantes, dulcibus uerbis

underþeodde, facn piðinnan tyddriende, spa spa berȝyls
dediti, dolum intus alentes, sicut sepulchrum

metton oferȝepeorke, piþinnan full stence ?
depicto mausoleo, intus plenum fetore ?

Þe nellaþ spa pesan pise, forþam he nys pis, þe mid
Nolumus sic esse sapientes, quia non est sapiens, qui

dydrunȝe hyne sylfne bespicð. 260
simulatione semet ipsum decipit.

Ac hu pille ȝe ?
Sed quomodo uultis ?

Þe pyllaþ beon bylepite butan licetunȝe, 7 pise þæt pe
Uolumus esse simplices sine hipochrisi, et sapientes ut

buȝon fram yfele 7 don ȝoda. Ȝyt þeahhpæþere deoplicor
declinemus a malo et faciamus bona. Adhuc tamen profundius

mid us þu smeaȝst, þonne yld ure onfon mæȝe ; ac sprec
nobiscum disputas, quam etas nostra capere possit ; sed loquere

us æfter uran ȝepunon, næs spa deoplice. 265
nobis nostro more, non tam profunde.

7 ic do æal spa ȝe biddaþ. Þu, cnapa, hpæt dydest
Et ego faciam sicut rogatis. Tu, puer, quid fecisti

todæȝ ?
hodie ?

---

254 *uersipelles*] *uersi pelles*   **257** *facn*] *fan*   *tyddriende*] *tyddriende,*
altered from *tyddriene*   **258** *intus*] added above line   **259** *qui*
simulatione] *quasi mulatione*   **267** *todæȝ*] *dæȝ*

---

253 Þyllaþ : without the pron. Cf., however, 259, 262, for its
inclusion in the gloss.
255 *astuti* : Wright-Wülcker and Thorpe read *uafri* ; but as
Zupitza, *op. cit.* 42, points out, J also has *astuti*. Wright-Wülcker
punctuate with a comma after *uafri*, the above is the punctuation
of Zupitza and Stevenson. **257-8** A reference to Matt. xxiii. 27.

Maneʒa þinʒ ic dyde. On þisse niht, þa þa cnyll ic
Multas res feci.   Hac nocte, quando signum

ʒehyrde, ic aras on minon bedde 7 eode to cyrcean, 7 sanʒ
audiui, surrexi de lectulo et exiui ad ecclesiam, et cantaui

uhtsanʒ mid ʒebroþrum ; æfter þa þe sunʒon be eallum ²⁷⁰
nocturnam cum fratribus ; deinde cantauimus de omnibus

halʒum 7 dæʒredlice lofsanʒas ; æfter þysum prim 7 seofon
sanctis et matutinales laudes ; post hęc primam et VII

seolmas mid letanian 7 capitolmæssan ; syþþan undertide,
psalmos cum letaniis et primam missam ; deinde tertiam,

7 dydon mæssan be dæʒe ; æfter þisum þe sunʒan middæʒ,
et fecimus missam de die ; post hęc cantauimus sextam,

7 æton 7 druncon 7 slepon, 7 eft þe arison 7 sunʒon non ;
*et manducauimus et bibimus et dormiuimus, et iterum surreximus et
cantauimus nonam ;*

7 nu þe synd her ætforan þe, ʒearuþe ʒehyran hþæt þu us ²⁷⁵
et modo sumus hic coram te, parati audire quid nobis

²⁶⁹ cyrcean] cycean   ²⁷⁰ þe] þe, altered from po   ²⁷¹ lofsanʒas
lofsanʒes   ²⁷³ mæssan] mæssa   ²⁷⁴ druncon] drucon   nonam]
nouam

---

²⁷⁰ þa : acc. after æfter is rare. No doubt as Wyatt suggests,
the text originally had þá (þam).

²⁷¹ lofsanʒas : MS-es, which might be an example of the very
late nom.acc.pl. in es (Sievers(Cook) § 237 note 3). Owing to the
influence and zeal of S. Benedict of Aniane, the monasteries of
Europe in the ninth century added to the prescribed divine
supplementary devotions. Although opposed at the Council of
Aachen (817), these devotional accretions took deep root ; ' not
only do we find everywhere daily said in the monasteries, in the
second half of the ninth century, the fifteen psalms introduced by
Benedict before matins, as well as the matins, lauds and vespers
of the dead, but also a new devotional office the vespers and lauds
of All Saints, and the seven penitential psalms and litany introduced after prime (E. Bishop, *The Origin of the Prymer*, EETS
(Orig. Series) CIX. xxi). Cf. G. G. Coulton, *op. cit.* I. 213 ff, 231 ff.

²⁷⁴ The monks eat nothing before noon, and the school is held
in the late afternoon, but as for the boys, ' if any be so young and
tender that he needs it, let bread and wine be brought to him at
daybreak as he sits in the cloister ' (G. G. Coulton, *op. cit.* I. 226,
quoting from E. Martène, *De antiquis Monachorum Ritibus* V. v.
230 ff.) Dr. Coulton's extracts provide a vivid picture of the life
of oblate children in the monastery.

secʒe.
dixeris.

Hpænne pylle ʒe synʒan æfen oþþe nihtsanʒc ?
Quando uultis cantare uesperam aut completorium ?

Þonne hyt tima byþ.
Quando tempus erit.

Þære þu todæʒ bespuncʒen ?
Fuisti hodie uerberatus ?

Ic næs, forþam pærlice ic me heold.   **280**
Non fui, quia caute me tenui.

7 hu þine ʒeferan ?
Et quomodo tui socii ?

Hpæt me ahsast be þam ?   Ic ne dear yppan þe diʒla ure.
Quid me interrogas de hoc ?   Non audeo pandere tibi secreta nostra.

Anra ʒehpylc þat ʒif he bespuncʒen pæs oþþe na.
Unusquisque scit si flagellatus erat an non.

Hpæt ytst þu on dæʒ ?
Quid manducas in die ?

---

[277] *uesperam]* *uesperum*   [279] *bespuncʒen]* the first *n* altered from *c*
[281] *dear]* *deor*

---

[279] *bespuncʒen :* ' if the boys offend in psalmody or chant, or
fall asleep, or in any other such transgression, forthwith and without delay they are stripped of frock and cowl and judged, and
beaten in their bare shirt, either by the prior or by their own
master, with smooth and supple osier rods kept for this single
purpose . . . the boys are scourged customarily, when there is
need, during talking-hour in cloister, never after vespers ' (Coulton,
op. cit. I. 225, from Martène).

[281] *Ic ne dear :* ' espionage and the rod were the two pillars of
monastic and scholastic discipline in the Middle Ages ' (Coulton,
A Medieval Garner 36). ' One boy accuseth another, if he knoweth
aught against him ; or, if he be found to have purposely concealed
anything, he is beaten as well as the offender (Coulton, *op. cit.* I.
226, from Martène : cf. 231 note 4). In one of Bata's colloquies
(Stevenson, 61) two boys who have been stealing apples from the
monastery orchard are shamelessly betrayed by their fellows, when
the master asks the class for information (cf. R. S. Rait, *Life in the
Medieval University* (Cambridge 1912) 108, on the *lupi* or *signatores*
of German Universities in the sixteenth century).

Ჳyt flæscmettum ic bruce, forðam cild ic eom under [285]
Adhuc carnibus uescor, quia puer sum sub

ჳyrda drohtniende.
uirga degens.

Hpæt mare ytst þu?
Quid plus manducas?

Ᵽyrta 7 æiჳra, fisc 7 cyse, buteran 7 beana 7 ealle clæne
Holera et oua, pisces et caseum, butirum et fabas et omnia munda

þinჳc ic ete mid micelre þancunჳe.
manduco cum gratiarum actione.

Spyþe paxჳeorn eart þu þonne þu ealle þinჳc etst þe þe [290]
Ualde edax es cum omnia manducas que tibi

toforan.
apponuntur.

Ic ne eom spa micel spelჳere þæt ic ealle cynn metta on
Non sum tam uorax ut omnia genera ciborum in

anre ჳereordinჳe etan mæჳe.
una refectione edere possim.

Ac hu?
Sed quomodo?

[290] *paxჳeorn*] *paxჳeorn*   [292] *genera*] above this word a gloss
has been erased : *cynn* is above *omnia*   [293] *possim*] *possum*

---

[285] *flæscmettum : brucan* is followed here by the dat. as in 184.
Wright-Wülcker think there is an error here, ' for the child evidently means to say, not that he eat [*sic*] meat, but that he did
not eat meat, because he was as yet too young '.   But the point
is that the boy is, as yet, a novice and therefore *may* eat butcher's
meat (*quadripedum carnes*) forbidden by the Rule (cap. 39–40)
to the monk, who, as Coulton, *op. cit.* I. 378, puts it, ' was too
often tempted to cry out, with those Israelites in the Wilderness,
" our soul loatheth this light bread ; who shall give us flesh to
eat ? " '

[287] *ytst :* cf. Sievers(Cook) § 371 note 3 (cf. *etst* [290])

[288] ' S. Benedict instituted something like strict vegetarianism
as a moral safeguard ' (Coulton, *op. cit.* I. 319, 376). *æiჳra*, Bülbring § 505, Sievers(Cook) § 290.

[290] *edax (paxჳeorn) :* for the application of this gloss to the
interpretation of *Beowulf* 3115, cf. notes thereon in the editions of
Chambers and Klaeber. Cf. also O. Schlutter, *Anglia* xxi. 527.

[291] sc. ჳesette synd.

Ic bruce hpilon þisum mettum,   oþrum mid [295]
Uescor aliquando his cibis, et aliquando aliis cum

syfernysse, spa spa dafnað munuce, næs mid oferhropse,
sobrietate, sicut decet monachum, non cum uoracitate,

forþam ic eom nan ʒluto.
quia non sum gluto.

7 hpæt drincst þu ?
Et quid bibis ?

Ealu, ʒif ic hæbbe, oþþe pæter ʒif ic næbbe ealu.
Ceruisam, si habeo, uel aquam si non habeo ceruisam.

Ne drincst þu pin ?   [300]
Nonne bibis uinum ?

Ic ne eom spa spediʒ þæt ic mæʒe bicʒean me pin ;
Non sum tam diues ut possim emere mihi uinum ;

7 pin nys drenc cilda ne dysʒra, ac ealdra 7 pisra.
et uinum non est potus puerorum siue stultorum, sed senum et
sapientium.

[295] *bruce*] *bruc*, the *e* covered by mounting of leaf   *Uescor*] *uesco*,
the *r* covered by mounting of leaf
[299] *næbbe*] *hæbbe   ealu*] *eala*   [300] *drincst*] *drncst*

---

[295] sc. *hpilon.   Uescor :* glossed in J by *ic beo ʒereordod.*

[296] *oferhropse :* etymology doubtful. H. Leo, *Angelsächsisches Glossar* (Halle 1872), suggests possibly connected with OE *crop*, ' crop (of a bird) '. F. Holthausen, *Altenglisches etymologisches Wörterbuch* (1934), has '*oferhrops*, Gierigkeit, zu *hrespan ?* ', which does not suit the required meaning. Is it possible that with the metathesis (Bülbring § 520) the form is related to NED *rasp* [2], *rosp* (cf. E. Anglian dial. *rasp*, belch) ?

[297] *gluto :* the gloss having already used *spelʒere* [292], lifts this word from the Latin, thus foreshadowing its future adoption into English from OFr (ME *glutun*).

[299] *ealu :* MS *eala*, possibly because of the frequent occurrence of *eala* (1, &c.)

[301] The Rule allowed the oblates ¼ lb. of bread and a little wine in the morning ; in England, where all wine was imported, the boys were apparently not so fortunate. The daily allowance for the monks was a *hemina*, probably as much as a pint.

[302] Glosses in J *drænc, ac ealdra.* At this point, in J, the master passes on to discuss gardening, and the pupil gives a long catalogue of trees and plants. Most of this occurs again in another of Bata's

47

Hpær slæpst ?
Ubi dormis ?

On slæpern mid ӡebroþrum.
In dormitorio cum fratribus.

Hpa apecþ þe to uhtsancӡe ?   305
Quis excitat te ad nocturnos ?

Hpilon ic ӡehyre cnyll 7 ic arise ; hpilon lareop min
Aliquando audio signum et surgo ; aliquando magister meus

apecþ me stiþlice mid ӡyrde.
excitat me duriter cum uirga.

Eala, ӡe cildra 7 pynsume leorneras, eop manaþ eoper
O, probi pueri et uenusti mathites, uos hortatur uester

lareop þæt ӡe hyrsumian ӡodcundum larum 7 þæt ӡe
eruditor ut pareatis diuinis disciplinis et

healdan eop sylfe ænlice on ælcere stope. Ꝺaþ þeaplice 310
obseruetis uosmet eleganter ubique locorum. Inceditis morigerate

þonne ӡe ӡehyran cyricean bellan, 7 ӡaþ into cyrcean,
cum auscultaueritis ecclesie campanas, et ingredimini in orationem,

7 abuӡaþ eadmodlice to halӡum pefodum, 7 standaþ
et inclinate suppliciter ad almas aras, et state

þeaplice, 7 sinӡað anmodlice, 7 ӡebiddaþ for eoprum
disciplinabiliter, et concinite unanimiter, et interuenite pro uestris

---

³⁰⁴ *fratribus*] *fribus*, with no abbrev. sign   ³⁰⁶ *arise*] *crise*
³⁰⁷ *uirga*] *uirga*, altered from *uirgo*   ³⁰⁸ *mathites*] *machites* *uester*]
uestes

---

colloquies (Stevenson, 58 ff) and derives from Ælfric's *Glossary*
(ed. Zupitza, 310 ff). The section is interesting for the numerous
OE glosses which have been added in J.

³⁰⁶ *arise* : Wyatt, *Anglo-Saxon Reader* 220, following Wright-
Wülcker, says the MS has *erise*, adding that this form suggests
the weakening and probably the shortening of the prefix at this
date. The MS, however, has plainly *crise* for normal *arise*.

³¹⁰ *ænlice* : Sievers(Cook) § 100 note 3.

³¹¹ *cyrcean* : Zupitza, *op. cit.* 45, notices that this is not an exact
gloss for *orationem*.

48

synnum, 7 ȝaþ ut butan hyȝeleaste to claustre oþþe to
erratibus, et egredimini sine scurrilitate in claustrum uel in
leorninȝa. 315
gimnasium.

---

314 *sine*] *siue*   *scurrilitate*] *scirilitatem*   315 *leorninȝa*] *leorninȝc*

---

314 *hyȝeleaste :* cf. Introd., and Bernard of Besse (quoted by
Coulton, *Ten Medieval Studies* 45), ' let not novices be easily moved
to laughter, tittering in general is a great disgrace to the gravity
of a religious '. Cf. also Alcuin's letter to Eanbald, Archbishop of
York, Migne, *Patrologia Latina* c. 224 f (Epist. lvi).

315 *leorninȝa :* MS *leorninȝc*. Is it possible that the gloss was
originally *leorninȝhuse*, which occurs in Wright-Wülcker 184/10
as the gloss to *gymnasium* ? Perhaps the spelling *inȝ* as against
unȝ (cf. 7) supports this (cf. Luick § 328 Anm.). In Bata's *Colloquia
Difficiliora* (Stevenson, 70), the pupils (*sollertissimę apes spiritalium
rerum*) are told *apiarum uestrum est gymnasium uestrum.*

BIBLIOGRAPHY

FACSIMILE

1901 H. D. Traill and J. S. Mann, *Social England* (illustrated ed), I,
p. 189 (fol. 61b).

EDITIONS

1830 A. Gurney in H. S. English, *Ancient History, English and French,
exemplified in a Regular Dissection of the Saxon Chronicle*,
pp. 226-39.

1834 B. Thorpe, *Analecta Anglo-Saxonica*, pp. 101-18; 2nd ed. 1846,
pp. 18-36.

1835 H. Leo, *Altsächsische und angelsächsische Sprachproben*, pp.
1-11; 2nd ed. 1838, pp. 6-15.

1847 F. W. Ebeling, *Angelsæchsisches Lesebuch*, pp. 46-57.

1849 L. F. Klipstein, *Analecta Anglo-Saxonica*, I, pp. 195-214.

1855 T. Müller, *Angelsächsisches Lesebuch*, pp. 14-32.

1857 T. Wright, *Anglo-Saxon and Old English Vocabularies*, I, cols.
1-14; 2nd ed. R. P. Wülcker, cols. 89-103.

1876 F. A. March, *Anglo-Saxon Reader*, pp. 13-22.

1929 W. H. Stevenson, *Early Scholastic Colloquies*, pp. 75-102.

Extracts can be found in various Old English primers.

TRANSLATIONS

1908 A. S. Cook and C. B. Tinker, *Select Translations from Old English Prose*, pp. 177-86.

1912 S. H. Gem, *An Anglo-Saxon Abbot: Ælfric of Eynsham*, pp.
183-95.

1916 A. R. Benham, *English Literature from Widsith to the Death of
Chaucer: A Source Book*, pp. 26-34.

1975 M. J. Swanton, *Anglo-Saxon Prose*, pp. 107-15.

Extracts can be found in various social and literary histories.

BIBLIOGRAPHY

STUDIES AND NOTES

1880 J. Zupitza, *Ælfrics Grammatik und Glossar*.

1885 E. M. Thompson, 'Ælfric's Vocabulary', Journal of the British Archaeological Association, xli 144-52.

1887 J. Zupitza, 'Die ursprüngliche Gestalt von Ælfrics Colloquium', ZfdA, xxxi 32-45.

1897 E. Schröder, 'Colloquium Ælfrici', ZfdA, xli 283-90.

1898 C. L. White, *Ælfric: A New Study of his Life and Writings* (Yale Studies in English 2).

1900 A. S. Napier, *Old English Glosses, chiefly unpublished*.

1903 R. Jordan, *Die altenglischen Säugetiernamen*.

1906 J. d. Z. Cortelyou, *Die altenglischen Namen der Insekten, Spinnen- und Krustentiere* (Anglistische Forschungen 19).

1906 J. J. Köhler, *Die altenglischen Fischnamen* (Anglistische Forschungen 21).

1907 C. H. Whitman, 'The Old English animal names: mollusks; toads; frogs; worms; reptiles', Anglia, xxx 380-93.

1943 M. M. Dubois, *Ælfric; Sermonnaire, Docteur et Grammairien*.

1943 L. Whitbread, 'Notes on Ælfric's Colloquy', Notes and Queries, clxxxiv 69-71.

1959 P. Clemoes, 'The chronology of Ælfric's works', in *The Anglo-Saxons: Studies presented to Bruce Dickins*, pp. 212-47.

1959 G. N. Garmonsway, 'The development of the colloquy', *ibidem*, pp. 248-61.

1961 E. Colledge, 'An allusion to Augustine in Ælfric's Colloquy', Review of English Studies, NS xii 180-81.

1963 H. Fujiwara, 'On the infinitive in the interlinear gloss of Ælfric's Colloquy', Anglica, v 10-22.

1966 P. Clemoes, 'Ælfric', in *Continuations and Beginnings*, ed. E. G. Stanley, pp. 176-209.

1972 D. A. Bullough, 'The educational tradition in England from Alfred to Ælfric: teaching *utriusque linguae*', Settimane di studio del Centro Italiano di Studi sull' Alto Medioevo, xix 453-94.

1972 J. Hurt, *Ælfric*.

1974 E. R. Anderson, 'Social idealism in Ælfric's Colloquy', Anglo-Saxon England, ii 153-62.

1986 R. Nagueka, 'Complementation in Ælfric's Colloquy', in *Linguistics across Historical and Geographical Boundaries: in Honour of Jacek Fisiak*, pp. 533-45.

1987 L. M. Reinsma, *Ælfric, an Annotated Bibliography*.

GLOSSARY

For the abbreviations and arrangement of the Glossary, see *Deor* (ed. Kemp Malone) p. 35, or *The Parker Chronicle* (ed. A. H. Smith), p. 56.

A

ăbūgan, *v.(2)*, [ABOW]; bow 312

ac, *conj.* [AC]; but 9

ăcennan, *w.v.(1b)*, produce 155

ădrēogan, *v.(2)*, [ADREE]; endure 186

ădrīfan, adrīfaδ 194, adryfaδ 200 (*pres.pl.*), *v.(1)*, drive

ăfandian, *w.v.(2)* prove 203

ăfēdan, ăfēst (*2sg.pres.*), 137, *w.v.(1b)*, feed

ăgēnlǣdan, *w.v.(1b)*, [AGAIN + LEAD]; lead back 39

ăhsian, ăhsie (*1sg.pres.*), 204, **ăhsige** 249, **ăxie** 11; *w.v.(2)*, ASK

ăn, **ǣnne** (*acc.sg.m.*), 51, *adj. pron.* ONE 293; A, AN 232; *ănra gehwylc* 235, each one; *þæt ăn* 146 n, 183 n,

ancgel 221, **ancgil** 91, *m.a-stem*, [ANGLE]; hook

and, (*denoted by* 7), *conj.* AND 2; *ond ... ond* 41, both ... and

andgyt, *n.a-stem*, [A N G I T]; understanding 247

ănmōdlīce, *adv.* together, with one accord 313

geanwyrde, *adj.* professed 13

ărīsan, *v.(1)*, ARISE 274

ărsmiδ, *m.a-stem*, [ORE + SMITH]; brass-smith, coppersmith 206

ăstīgan, *v.(1)*, 153; **ăstīgian**, *w.v.(2)* 91, [ASTYE]; go on board

ăweccan, *w.v.(1c)*, [AWECCHE]; awaken, arouse 305

Æ

æcer, *m.a-stem*, ACRE; field 27

ǣfen, *n.m.ja-stem*, EVEN; vespers 277

æfter, *prep.(with dat.)*, AFTER 271; according to 246; *æ. þa (acc.)* 270, after these

ǣig, **ǣigra** (*pl.*), *n.os-stem*, EGG 288

æl, *m.a-stem*, AWL 222

ǣl, *m.a-stem*, EEL 101

ǣlc, *pron.* EACH; every 188; all 189

ǣlepūta, *f.n-stem*, EEL-POUT; burbot, blenny 101

ǣmtig, *adj.* EMPTY 189

ǣnig, *pron.,adj.* ANY 28; *on ǣnigon* 192, in any way

ǣnlīce, *adv.* ONLY; decorously 310

ǣr, *n.a-stem*, ORE; brass 160

ǣrnemergen, *m.a-stem*, dawn 46

ǣs, *n.a-stem*, bait 92

æt, *prep.(with dat.)*, AT 25

ætberstan, *v.(3)*, [ATBURST]; escape 119

ætforan, *prep.(with dat.)*, [ATFORE]; before, in the presence of 275

ætwesan, *anom.v.* be present 183

ætwindan, *v.(3)*, [ATWIND]; escape 139

B

bæcere, *m.jo-stem*, BAKER 185

băr, *m.a-stem*, BOAR 66

be, *prep.(with dat.)*, BY; with 80; about 270; for 273

52

bĕah, *m.a-stem*, [BEE²] ; ring, armlet 84

bĕan, *f.ō-stem*, BEAN 288

bĕatan, *v.*(7), BEAT 228

becuman, *v.*(4), [BECOME] ; come 58

bedd, *n.ja-stem*, BED 269

bedrīfan, *v.*(1), drive 75

begān, begǣst (*2sg.pres.*), 22 ; *anom.v.*, [BEGO] ; practise 241; perform 22

began(c)gan, *v.*(7), pursue, practise 85, 238

begrynian, begrynodo (*p.part. neut.pl.*) 60 ; *w.v.*(2), [BE + GRIN] ; ensnare

begytan, *v.*(5), [BEGET] ; get, acquire 88

behĕfe, *adj.* [BIHEVE] ; useful 6

behwyrfan, *w.v.*(1b), instruct, exercise 241

belle, *w.f.* BELL 311

bĕod, *m.a-stem*, [BEOD] ; table 189

bĕon ; bĕo (*1sg.pres.*) ; blŏ 201, byŏ (*3sg.pres.*) 190 ; bĕoð, bĕo (*pres.pl.*) 201 ; bĕo (*imp.sg.*) 242; bī (*pres.subj.*) 10; *anom.v.*, BE

gebeorhlic, *adj.* safe 112

beran, *v.*(4), BEAR ; carry 33

bergyls, *m.a-stem*, [BURIELS] ; tomb, sepulchre 257

besencean, *w.v.*(1a), [BESENCH]; sink 118

beswīcan, *v.*(1), [BESWIKE] ; deceive 260 ; ensnare 124

beswin(c)gan, *v.*(3), [BE-SWINGE] ; beat, flog 8

betǣcan, *w.v.*(1c), [BETEACH] ; show, point 64 ; hand over

betwēnan, *adv.* BETWEEN ; in the meantime 15

betweoh 213, betwux 211 ; *prep.*(*with dat.*), BETWIXT ; among

beðurfan, *pret.pres.*(3), need 192

bicgean 301, gebicgan 164, bigŏ (*pres.*) 98 ; *w.v.*(1c), BUY

biddan, *v.*(5), BID ; ask, request 1

gebiddan, *v.*(5), BID ; pray 313

biggencere, *m.ja-stem*, worker 207

bigleofa, *m.n-stem*, [BYLIVE, BY-LIFE] ; food 236

bilewit 9, bylewit 262 ; *adj.*, [BILEWHIT] ; kind 9, sincere 262

binne, *w.f.* BIN, manger 32 n

blāwan, *v.*(7), BLOW, *v*¹ 228

bliss, *f.jo-stem*, BLISS ; satisfaction 176

brǣdan, *w.v.*(1b), [BREDE, *v*¹] ; roast, broil 199

brēdan, *v.*(3), [BREDE, *v*²] ; knot, weave 57

bridd, *m.ja-stem*, young BIRD ; 139

brīdelŏwancg, *m.a-stem*,BRIDLE + THONG ; rein 172

broð, *n.a-stem*, BROTH 196

gebrŏðor, *m.r-stem*, BROTHER ; brother-monk, brethren (*pl.*) 14

brūcan, brȳcð (*pres.*) 177 ; *v.*(2), enjoy 177 ; [BROOK] ; use 184 ; partake of 285

būgan, *v.*(2), BOW ; depart 263

būton, būtan 314 ; *prep.* [BOUT, BUT] ; without 314 ; *conj.* provided that 5 ; unless 10 ; except 61

butere, *f.n-stem*, BUTTER 41

butergeŏwĕor, *n.a-stem*, butter-curd, butter 182

buteric, *m.a-stem*, leather-bottle 172

bylig, *m.a-stem*, BELLY ; bellows 228

bysgian, *w.v.*(2), BUSY; occupy, employ 14

C

capitolmæsse, *f.n-stem*, chapter-mass 272

ceaster, *f.o-stem*, [CHESTER]; city 97

ceasterware (*pl.*), *f.ō-stem*, citizens 99

ceorl, *m.a-stem*, CHURL; freeman, peasant 241

cild, **cīld** (*pl.*) 244, **cīldra** 308, **cīlda** (*gen.pl.*) 302; *n.os-stem*, CHILD, boy 285

cin(c)g(c), *m.a-stem*, KING 55

clǣne, *adj.* CLEAN (in the initial sense) 95 n

clauster, *n.a-stem*, CLOISTER 314

cleafa, *m.n-stem*, [CLEVE²]; cellar 181

c n a p a, *m.n-stem*, [K N A P E], *KNAVE*; boy 266

cnyll, *m.ja-stem*, *KNELL*; sound of a bell 268

crabba, *m-n-stem*, CRAB 106

cræft, *m.a-stem*, CRAFT; occupation, calling 56

culter, *m.a-stem*, COULTER 26

cunnan, **cann** (*1sg.pres.*) 130, **canst** (*2sg.pres.*) 86, **cūþe** (*1sg.pret.*) 130, *pret.-pres.* (3), CAN *v*¹; know how to 130, know 9, be conversant with 86

cwic, *adj.* QUICK; alive 157

gecwylman, *w.v.*(1b) destroy, kill 118

cyldu, *w.f.*, [CHELDE]; cold 30

cyle, *m.i-stem*, CHILL; cold 38

cynn, *n.ja-stem*, [KIN]; kind, sort 171

cȳpan, *w.v.*(1b), [CHEAP]; sell 96

cȳpmann, *m.monos.stem*, CHAPMAN; merchant 20

cyr(i)ce, *f.n-stem*, CHURCH 269

cȳse, *m.ja-stem*, CHEESE 41

cȳsgerunn, *n.i-stem*, cheese-curd 182

D

dafnian, *w.v.*(2), beseem, befit 296

dæg, *m.a-stem*, DAY 13; *on dæg* 284, during the day

dægrǣd, *n.a-stem*, [DAY-RED]; dawn 23

dægrēdlic, *adj.* matutinal 271

dǣl, *m.i-stem*, [DEAL]; region; *sǣlice dǣlas* 154, the high seas

dēoplīce, **dēoplīcor** (*comp.*) 263; *adv.* DEEPLY; profoundly 265

gedeorf, *n.a-stem*, [DERF]; labour, toil 36

deorfan, **gedeorfan** 44; *v.*(3), [DERVE]; labour 23

dēorwyrðe, **dȳr-** 154; *adj.* [DEARWORTH]; precious, valuable 159

dīgol, *n.a-stem*, [DIGHEL]; secret 282

dōn, **dō** (*1sg.pres.*) 32, **dēst** (*2sg. pres.*) 31, **dōð** (*pres.pl.*) 146, **dyde**, (*1sg.pret.*) 268, **dydest** (*2sg.pret.*), **dydon** (*pret.pl.*) 273; *anom.v.* DO 32, make 41

drenc, *m.i-stem*, DRENCH; drink 226

drīfan, *v.*(1), DRIVE 37

drincan, *v.*(3), DRINK 274

drohtnian, *w.v.*(2), conduct oneself, behave, live 286

durran, **dear** (*pres.*) 282, **durre** (*pres.subj.*) 25; *pret.pres.*(3), DARE

dydrung, *f.ō-stem*, delusion 260

dyrstig, *adj.* venturesome, daring 74

dysig, *adj.* DIZZY; foolish (ones) 302

E

ēa, *f.monos.stem*, [EA] ; river 91

ēac, *adv.*, [EKE] ; also ; *e. swylce* 19, also

ēadmōdlīce, *adv.*, [EDMOD-LICHE] ; humbly, reverently 312

eala, *interj.* O ! 1

ealu, *n.þ-stem*, ALE 299

eald, *adj.*, [ELD, *a*] ; *OLD* 302

ealdordōm, *m.a-stem*, [ALDER-DOM] ; pre-eminence 217

ealdorscype, *m.i-stem*, [ALDER-SHIP] ; supremacy, sovereignty 214

eall ; *adj.* ALL 45, **eall**, *adv.* altogether ; *æal swa*, just as 266, at the price 162

efne, *adv.* EVEN ; *interj.* lo ! 182

eft, *adv.* [EFT] ; again 46 ; thereafter, afterwards 144

ege, *m.i-stem*, AWE, fear 25

ēhtan, *w.v.(1b)* pursue, chase 58

ele, *m.i-stem*, *OIL* 160

eoldormann, *m.monos.stem*, ALDERMAN ; ruler, nobleman 150

eom (*1sg.pres.*) 42 ; **eart** (*2sg.pres.*) 242 ; **ys** (*3sg.pres.*) 8 ; **synt** (*pres.pl.*) 18, **synd** 198, **syndon** 2 ; **sȳ** (*pres.subj.*) 6 ; *anom.v.* AM, ART, IS, &c.

eorōtilō, *f.ō-stem*, [EARTH-TILTH] ; agriculture 219

erian, *w.v.(2)*, [EAR, *v*¹] ; plough 27

etan 293 ; **ete** (*1sg.pres.*) 289 ; **etst** (*2sg.pres.*) 290, **ytst** 287 ; **etaō** (*pres.pl.*) 195 ; **ǣton** (*pret.pl.*) 274 ; *v.(5)* EAT

F

fācn, *n.a-stem*, [FAKEN] ; deceit, guile 257

fagc, *f.ō-stem*, plaice 107

faran, *v.(6)* FARE, go 113

fǣrlīce, *adv.* [FEAR + LY²] ; suddenly, quickly 76

fæstnian, *w.v.(2)*, FASTEN ; fix 26

fæt, *n.a-stem*, VAT, vessel, utensil 230

fǣtels, *m.a-stem*, vessel 174

fǣtt, *adj.* FAT ; rich 196

fe(a)la, *adj.indecl.* [FELE] ; many 99

fēdan, *w.v.(1b)*, FEED 84

fēld, *m.u-stem*, FIELD 24

fell, *n.a-stem*, FELL ; skin 170

feoh, *n.a-stem*, FEE ; money 89

gefēra, *m.n-stem*, [YFERE] ; companion 17

gefērscipe, *m.i-stem*, fellowship, society 194

fisc, **fixas** 90 (*pl.*) *m.a-stem*, FISH, *sb*¹, 116

fiscere, *m.ja-stem*, FISHER, fisherman 19

fixian, *w.v.(2)*, FISH 103

flǣscmete, *m.i-stem*, FLESH-MEAT ; meat 195

flaxe, *f.n-stem*, FLASK, *sb*² ; bottle 172

geflit, *n.a-stem*, dispute 234

flōc, *n.(?)a-stem*, FLUKE, *sb*¹ ; flat fish, flounder 107

foddor, *n.a-stem*, FODDER 237

folc, **folce** 151 (*dat.sg.*) ; *n.a-stem*, FOLK ; people

gefōn ; **gefeo** 66, **gefō** (*1sg.pres.*) 81, **gefēhst** (*2sg.pres.*) 65, **gefōō** (*pres.pl.*) 119, **gefēngc** (*1sg.pret.*) 73, **gefēncge** (*2sg. pret.*) 72 ; *v.(7)*, [FANG] ; catch

for, *prep.(with dat. or acc.)*, FOR 46 ; on account of 30

forbīgean, *w.v.(1b)*, despise, shun 191

forewerd, *adj.* [FORWARD] ; early 37

forhtfull, *adj.* fainthearted, timid 78

GLOSSARY

forhwī, *interr.adv.*, [FORWHY]; why 249

forlǣtan, *v.*(7), [FORLET]; neglect, forsake 239; let 141

forlidenes, *f.jō-stem*, shipwreck 156

forswelgan, *v.*(3), [FORSWAL-LOW]; devour 39

forðām, forðāmðe, *conj.* because, since 2

forōtēon, forōtȳhst 246 (*2sg. pres.*), *v.*(2) [FORTHTEE] draw forth; *f. sprǣce* 246, speak

forōȳ, *conj.* [FORTHY]; therefore 200

fracod, *adj.* [FRAKED]; base, impious 6

fram, *prep.*(*with dat.*), FROM 194; by 10

fram, *adv.* FROM; away 200

frēcnys, *f.jō-stem*, peril, danger 119

fremman (fremian), framīge 235 (*sg.pres.subj.*), **fremode** 163 (*sg.pret.subj.*); *w.v.*(1a), [FREME]; benefit, help 163

frēoh, *adj.* FREE 35

fugelere, *m.ja-stem*, FOWLER 20

fugol, fugelas (*pl.*) 124; *m.a-stem*, FOWL; bird

full, *adj.* FULL, filled 258; entire, whole 27

furōon, *adv.* [FORTHEN]; even 191; *ne f. þæt an* 183 n, not even

furōra, *adj.comp.* FURTHER; greater, superior 212

fyllan, gefyllan, *w.v.*(1b), FILL 32; replenish 181

fyrmest, *adj.* FOREMOST; first 215

fȳrspearca, *m.n-stem*, fire-spark 227

'G

gegaderungc, *f.ō-stem*, GATHER-ING, community 209

gādīsen, *n.ja-stem*, GOAD + IRON; goad 29

gān, gāð 310 (*imper.*), **ēode** 269 (*3sg.pret.*); *anom.v.* GO

gærs, *n.a-stem*, GRASS 251

gē; ēow (*acc.*) 249; **ēower** (*gen.*) 201; **ēow** (*dat.*) 183; *pron.* YE 4

ge, *conj.* [YE]; and, also; *ge . . . ond* 150, both . . . and

gēa, *interj.* YEA 37

gearkian, *w.v.* (2), [YARK]; prepare, 170

gearu, *adj.* [YARE]; ready 145

geornlīce, *adv.* [YERNLY]; diligently 238

gif, *conj.* IF 94

gistlīðe, *adj.* hospitable 177

glæs, *n.a-stem*, GLASS 161

'gluto', 297; glutton

God, *m.n.a-stem*, GOD 213

gōd, *adj.* GOOD 204

gōd, *n.a-stem*, GOOD (thing) 263

godcund, *adj.* [GODCUND]; sacred, divine 309

godspell, *n.a-stem*, GOSPEL 214

gōld, *n.a-stem*, GOLD 159

gōldsmiō, golsmiō 231, *m.a-stem*, GOLDSMITH 205

grēne, *adj.* GREEN, raw 195

grin, *n.i-stem*, [GRIN]; snare 125

gymm, *m.a-stem*, GEM, jewel 159

gyrd, *f.jo-stem*, YARD, *sb*²; rod 307

gyrstandæg, *m.a-stem*, YESTER-DAY 68

gȳt, *adv.* YET, as yet 285, still 263

H

habban, hæbbe (*1sg.pres.*) 29, **hæfst** (*2sg.pres.*) 28, **habbaō** (*pres.pl.*) 237, **habban** (*pres. subj.pl.*) 145, *w.v.*(3), HAVE

hacod, *m.a-stem*, HAKED, HACOT; pike, mullet 101

hafoc, *m.a-stem*, HAWK 126

hālga, *m.n-stem*, [HALLOW, *sb*¹] ; saint 271

hālig, *adj.* HOLY 312

hām, *m.a-stem*, HOME 25

hara, *m.n-stem*, HARE 66

hās, *adj. HOARSE* 30

gehæftan, *w.v.(1b)*, imprison, catch 92

hælfter, *f.ō-stem*, HALTER 173

gehæp, *adj.*, convenient 57

hærfæst, *m.a-stem*, HARVEST, autumn 140

hǣrincg, *m.a-stem*, HERRING 106

hǣtu, *f.ō-stem*, HEAT 38

hē ; hēo (*f.nom.sg.*) 245 ; hit (*neut.nom.sg.*) 5, hyt 34 ; hyne (*m.acc.sg.*) 75 ; his (*gen.sg.*) 238, hys 235 ; him (*dat.sg.*) 178 ; *pers.pron.* HE

healdan, heoldan 217, *v.*(7) HOLD

hebban, hæbbe (*1sg.pres.*) 41 ; *v.*(6), *HEAVE* ; lift, move

hēddern, *n.a-stem*, storehouse, storeroom 181

heort, *m.a-stem*, HART 66

heorte, *f.n-stem*, HEART 190

hēr, *adv.* HERE 162

hider, *adv.* HITHER 156

hīg, *n.ja-stem, HAY* 33

hig, *interj.* O ! 34

hig 138 ; hig (*acc.pl.*) 139, hī 98 ; heora (*gen.pl.*) 33 ; *pers. pron.* they

higdifæt, *n.a-stem*, leather-bottle 173

hindergēp, *adj.* [HINDERYEAP] ; wily, deceitful 256

hlæst, *n.a-stem*, [LAST, *sb*²] ; cargo, freight 153

hlāf, *m.a-stem*, LOAF 226

hlāford, *m.a-stem*, LORD, master 23

hors, *n.a-stem*, HORSE 84

hran, *m.a-stem*, whale 114

hrēam, *m.a-stem*, [REAM, *sb*¹] ; shouting 30

hrēaw, *adj.* RAW, uncooked 195

hū, *adv.* HOW 22

hund, *m.a-stem*, HOUND, dog, 39

hunta, *m.n-stem*, [HUNT, *sb*¹] ; huntsman 19

huntian, *w.v.(2)*, HUNT 61

huntnoð, *m.a-stem*, [HUNTETH] ; hunting 67

huntung, *f.ō-stem*, HUNTING 69 ; what is hunted, game 80

hūs, *n.a-stem*, HOUSE 230

hwā (*m.f.*) 305 ; hwæt (*neut.*) 4 ; hwæs (*gen.*) 54 ; hwām (*dat.*) 185 ; *pron.interr.* WHO, what

hwæl, hwælas (*pl.*) 119, *m.a-stem*, WHALE 109

hwænne, *adv.* WHEN 277

hwǣr, *adv.* WHERE 303

hwæðer, *conj.* WHETHER 185 ; swa h., 240 whichever ; h. þe, 134 or

hwætlīce, *adv.* [WHATLICHE] ; quickly 234

hwanon, *adv.*[WHENNE, WHEN]; whence 220

hwilc, 217, hwylc 180, wylc 102 ; *interr. pron., adj.* WHICH

hwīlon 66, hwȳlon 156 ; *adv. WHILOM* ; sometimes

hwistlung, *f.o-stem*, WHISTLING 126

gehwylc, *adj.pron.* each 235

gehwyrfan, *w.v.(1b)*, turn 190

hȳd, hȳda (*pl.*), *f.i-stem*, HIDE, *sb*¹, 170

hygelēast, *f.ō-stem*, jesting, buffoonery 314

hȳnð, *f.ō-stem*, humiliation, loss 242

gehȳran, *w.v.(1b)*, HEAR 275

hyrde, *m.ja-stem*, HERD ; custodian, keeper 183

hȳrsumian, *w.v.(2)*, [HEARSUM]; be obedient to 309

57

GLOSSARY

I

ic 11, **mē** (*dat.sg.*) 57 ; *pers.pron.* I, &c.

īdel, *adj.* IDLE ; foolish 6

intō, *prep.*(*with dat.*), INTO 311

īsen, **īsene** (*pl.*) 205, **īsenne** 227 ; *adj.* IRON

iukian, **iugie** (*1sg.pres.*) 24 ; *w.v.*(2), YOKE 26

K

kempa, *m.n-stem*, [KEMP] ; warrior 241

L

lamprede, *f.n-stem*, LAMPREY 101

láncge, *adv.* LONG 188

lánd, *n.a-stem*, LAND 155

lār, *f.ō-stem*, LORE ; precept 309

lārēow, *m.wa-stem*, [LAREW] ; teacher, master 1

gelǽccan, *w.v.*(*1c*), [LATCH, *v*¹] ; capture 70

lǽdan, **gelǽdan**, *w.v.*(*1b*), LEAD 45 ; bring 158

lǽs, *f.wō-stem*, [LEASE, *sb*¹] ; pasture 45

lǽtan, *s.v.*(7), LET, *v*¹ 139

lēasung, *f.ō-stem*, [LEASING] ; artifice, deceit 255

leax .*m.a-stem*, [LAX, *sb*¹] ; salmon 106

lēden, *adj.* [LEDEN] ; Latin 16

lencgten, *m.a-stem*, LENTEN ; spring 138

lēof *adj.* [LIEF] ; dear 23 ; (*comp.*) leofre ys us 8, we would rather ; *as noun*, leof, 37, geleof 35, sir !

leornere, *m.ja-stem*, LEARNER ; scholar 308

leornian, *w.v.*(2), LEARN 15

leornung 7, **-inga** (*dat.sg.*) 315 ; *f.ō-stem*, LEARNING ; study, meditation 315

letania, *m.n-stem*, LITANY 272

leðerhosu, *f.ō-stem*, leathern gaiter, leggings (*pl.*) 172

līcetung, *f.ō-stem*, deceit, hypocrisy 262

lician, *w.v.*(2), *impers.*, LIKE, *v*¹ ; please 245

līf, *n.a-stem*, LIFE 186

līm, *m.a-stem*, LIME ; bird-lime 125

lītlincg, *m.a-stem*, child 191

loc, *n.a-stem*, LOCK ; fold 41

lofsang, *m.a-stem*, [LOFSONG] ; song of praise, Lauds 271

lopystre, *f.n-stem*, LOBSTER 107

losian, *w.v.*(2), LOSE, *v*¹ ; perish, go bad 183

luflīce, *adv.* LOVELY ; dear 164n.

lustlīce, *adv.* willingly 85

lūtian, *w.v.*(2), [LOUT, *v*²] ; hide 25

lyre, *m.i-stem*, [LURE] ; loss 157

lȳt, **lǣs** (*comp.*) ; *adv.* [LITE] ; little ; þe læs 39, lest

lytig, *adj.* crafty 255

M

magan, **mæg** (*1.3sg.pres.*) 62, **miht** (*2sg.pres.*) 232, **magon** (*pres.pl.*) 187, **mǣge** (*pres. subj.sg.*) 264 ; *pret.pres.*(5), MAY, be able

mancgere, *m.ja-stem*, MONGER¹ ; trader, merchant 149

manian, *w.v.*(2), remind, exhort 308

manig 144, **mænig** 119, **manegum** (*dat.pl.*) 114 ; *adj.* MANY

man, *m.monos.stem*, MAN 190

max, *n.a-stem*, [MASK, *sb*¹, MESH] ; net 57

mægen, *n.a-stem*, MAIN, *sb*¹ ; strength 190

mæsse, *f.n-stem*, MASS 273

mæsseprēst, *m.a-stem*, MASS-PRIEST 240

mæstlingc, *n.a-stem*, [MASLIN¹];
brass 160

mǣð, *f.i-stem*, [METHE]; meas-
ure, ability 246

melkan, *v.(3)*, MILK 40

mereswȳn, *n.a-stem*, MERE-
SWINE; porpoise, dolphin 106

mētan, *w.v.(1b)*, [METE, *v*³];
paint 258

mete, mettas *(pl.)*, *m.i-stem*,
MEAT; food 95

micel, micclan *(dat.sg.)* 156,
māra *(comp.)* 136; *adj.*
[MICKLE]; great 289

mid, mit 27, *prep.(with dat.)*,
[MID]; with 29, to 27

middæg, *m.a-stem*, MIDDAY;
sext 273

mīn, mīnon *(dat.sg.m.)* 42,
mȳnan *(dat.sg.neut.)* 113;
poss.adj. MINE, my

mis(t)lic, *adj.* [MISLICH]; manifold 78, various 171, 230

mōd, *n.a-stem*, MOOD, *sb¹*; heart
121

morgen, *m.a-stem*, MORN 37

munuc, monuc 13; *m.a-stem*,
MONK 203

musle, *f.n-stem*, MUSSEL 107

myne, *m.i-stem*, MINNOW 101

N

nā, *adv.conj.* NO⁻; not 188; *n.*
þæt ān 117 *n.* 147 *n.*, not only

nabban, næbbe *(1sg.pres.)* 299;
w.v.(3), have not, lack

nān, *pron.adj.*, NONE 176, no 297

nǣdl, *f.ō-stem*, NEEDLE 222

næs, *adv.* not, not at all 6

ne, *adv.* not 8; *conj.* neither, nor
188

ne + wēsan; nēom *(1sg.pres.)*
35 (cf. 292); nys *(3sg.pres.)*
24, nis 222; næs *(3sg.pret.)*
68; *v.(5)* be not

nellan, nelle *(1sg.pres.)* 142,

nele *(3sg.pres.)* 174, nellað
(pres.pl.) 191; *anom.v.*
[NILL]; be unwilling

nēodðearf, *adj.* necessary 168

nett, nettum *(dat.pl.)* 61, -an 59,
neton 124; *n.ja-stem*, NET

nic, *adv.* not I, no 110

niht, *f.monos-stem*, NIGHT 45

nihtsangc, *m.a-stem*, compline
277

geniman, -nym-; *v.(4)*, [NIM];
take 93, keep 95, catch 139

nōn, *n.a-stem*, NOON; none 274

notian, *w.v.(2)*, [NOTE, *v¹*]; use
229

nū, *adv.* NOW 30

nȳten, *n.a-stem*, [NETEN]; beast,
cattle 250

nytenys, -ssæ *(dat.sg.)* 122;
f.jō-stem, cowardice

nytwyrðnes, -ssæ *(gen.sg.)* 167;
f.jō-stem, utility

O

O 146, see on

of, *prep.(with dat.)*, OF 48, from
88

ofer, *prep.(with acc.)*, OVER 38,
146; past 144; beyond 245

ofergeweork, *n.a-stem*, [OVER-
WORK]; superstructure, sepul-
chral monument 258

oferhrops, *f.ō-stem*, voracity 296

oferwintran, *w.v.(1b)*, [OVER-
WINTER]; get through the
winter 174

ofslēan, *v.(6)*, [OFSLAY]; slay
60

ofstikian, *w.v.(2)*, stab to death
76

on, o 146; *prep.(with dat. and
acc.)*; ON, in 14; at 292; *on
dæg* 31, in the day, daily;
on þærtō 41, in addition

onbelǣdan, *w.v.(1b)*, inflict
upon 9

ondswerian, *w.v.*(*2*), ANSWER 224

ondwyrdan, *w.v.*(*1b*), [AND-WURDE] ; answer 231

onfōn, *v.*(*7*), [ONFANG] ; take, receive 264

onglǽwlic, *adj.* artful 255

ostre, *f.n-stem*, OYSTER 106

ōðer, ōðron (*dat.pl.*) 235 ; *pron. adj.* OTHER

oððæt, *conj.* until 58

oððe, *conj.* or 6

oxa ; oxan (*acc.pl.*) 29, oxon 24 ; oxan (*gen.pl.*) 33, (*dat.pl.*) 26 ; *m.n-stem*, OX

oxanhyrde, *m.ja-stem*, OXHERD 18

P

pæll, *m.a-stem*, PALL, purple garment 159

pinne, *f.n-stem*, flask, bottle 173

pliht, *m.a-stem*, [PLIGHT] ; danger, risk 156

plyhtlic, *adj.* [PLIGHTLY] ; dangerous 112

prættig, *adj.* PRETTY ; sly, cunning 254

prīm, *?n.a-stem*, PRIME 271

pusa, *m.n-stem*, bag, scrip 173

R

rā, rānn (*pl.*) 66 ; *m.n-stem*, ROE[1]

gerǽdan, *w.v.*(*1b*), READ ; [*ys*]gerǽd 214, reads

gerǽde, *n.ja-stem*, trappings 172

rǽge, *f.n-stem*, doe, of the roe-deer 66

rēaf, *n.a-stem*, [REAF] ; garment 159

recc(e)an 197, rēc(e)an 5 ; *w.v.* (*1c*), RECK, care (for)

gereord, *f.ō-stem*, [RERDE] ; language 16

gereording 293, gererduncg 177, *f.ō-stem*, meal

rēwyt, *n.ja-stem*, rowing 104

rīce, *n.ja-stem*, [RICHE] ; kingdom 215

riht, *adj.* RIGHT, correct 5

rihtwīsnes, *f.jō-stem*, RIGHTEOUSNESS 215

rōwan, *s.v.*(*7*), ROW, *v*[1], sail 153

S

sang, *m.a-stem*, SONG, singing 15

sǽ, *m.f.i-stem*, SEA 103

sǽcocc, *m.a-stem*, cockle, shellfish 107

sǽlic, *adj.* of the sea, marine 153

sceamu, *f.ō-stem*, SHAME 242

scēap, *n.a-stem*, SHEEP 37

scē(a)phyrde, *m.ja-stem*, SHEPHERD 18, 36

scear, *m.n.a-stem*, SHARE, *sb*[1], ploughshare 26

scearn, *n.a-stem*, [SHARN] ; dung, muck 33

sceatt, *m.a-stem*, [SCAT, *sb*[1]] ; money, profit 120

sceōwyrhta 167, scē- 20, -wyrhton (*d.sg.*) 206, *m.n-stem*, [SHOE + WRIGHT] ; leather worker

sceōh, sceōs (*pl.*), *m.a-stem*, SHOE 171

sceota, *m.n-stem*, [SHOAT[1]] ; trout 101

scrūd, *n.monos-stem*, [SHROUD, *sb*[1]] ; clothing 89

scrȳdan, *w.v.*(*1b*), [SHRIDE, *v*[1]] ; clothe, dress 84

sculan, sceal (*1.3sg.pres.*) 78, sceoldon (*pret.pl.subj.*) 130 ; *pret.-pres.*(*4*), SHALL, have to, must ; hwæt sceoldon hig me 130, what use would they be to me ?

gescȳ, *n.pl.a-stem*, SHOES 171

scyp, *n.a-stem*, SHIP, boat 91

sĕ, *dem. pron.* that, it 239;
  þæt (*n. nom.*) 242, 243; þe
  (*instrum. with comp. adv.*)
  39, 85; þā (*acc.pl.*) 270 n;
  þām (*d.pl.*) 282

sĕ, *rel.pron.m.* who; þæne
  (*acc.sg.m.*) 116; þā (*n.pl*) 154,
  250

sĕ, *dem.adj.m.* this, that; þām
  (*m.dat.sg.*) 239

sĕ, *def.art.m.* the 44, &c.;
  þone (*m.acc.sg.*) 134; þæne,
  135, 136; þām (*m.dat.sg.*)
  47; þære (*f.dat.sg.*) 27; þā
  (*n.pl.*) 45; þām (*d.pl.*) 59, 60

sealt, *n.a-stem*, SALT 181

sealtere, -era 175; *m.ja-stem*,
  SALTER 21

sĕamere, *m.ja-stem*, tailor 222

sĕcean, *w.v.(1c)*, SEEK 215

secgan; secge (*1sg.pres.*) 150;
  segst (*2sg.pres.*) 122, sægst
  123, sægest 22; segð (*3sg.
  pres.*) 229, secgð 220, sægð
  233; secge (*pres.subj.*) 276;
  w.v.(3), SAY

selcūð, *adj.* [SELCOUTH]; rare,
  various 159

seldon, *adv.* SELDOM 104

seofon, *num.* SEVEN 13

seolm, *m.a-stem*, PSALM 272

seoloforsmið, *m.a-stem*, SILVER-
  SMITH 205

sĕon, *s.v.(5)*, SEE; pass. seem
  189

sĕoðan, *v.(2)*, [SEETHE]; boil
  198

settan, *w.v.(1a)*, SET 57

sibb, *f.jō-stem*, [SIB, *sb¹*]; peace,
  concord 234

sīde, *f.n-stem*, silk 159

sín(c)gan, sýngan 277; sún-
  gon (*pret.pl.*) 270, an 273; *v.
  (3)*, SING 13

slǣpan, *v.(7)*, SLEEP 274

slǣpern, *n.a-stem*, dormitory 304

alecg, *f.jo-stem*, SLEDGE, *sb¹*,
  sledge-hammer 228

slege, *m.i-stem*, blow 118

smĕag(e)an, *w.v.(2)*, deliberate;
  s. (*mid*) examine 264

smið, *m.a-stem*, SMITH 205,
  blacksmith 220

smiððe, *f.n-stem*, SMITHY 227

sōð, *n.a-stem*, [SOOTH]; truth
  121

sōðlīce, *adv.* [SOOTHLY]; truly
  188

spēdig, *adj.* [SPEEDY]; wealthy,
  rich 301

sp(r)æc, *f.jō-stem*, SPEECH 5;
  conversation 244

sp(r)ecan; sprycst (*2sg.pres.*)
  11; specst 248; sprecan
  (*pres.pl.subj.*) 5; sprec (*imper.*) 246; sprecende (*pres.
  part.*) 256; *v.(5)*, SPEAK

sprot, *f.ō-stem*, SPRAT, 102

spurleðer, *n.a-stem*, [SPUR-
  LEATHER]; spur-strap 173

spyrte, *f.n-stem*, wicker-basket,
  creel 92

standan, *v.(6)*, STAND 38

stearc, *adj.* STARK; severe 25

stenc, *m.i-stem*, STENCH 258

stiria, *m.n-stem*, sturgeon 106

stiðlīce, *adv.* sternly, forcibly
  307

stōw, *f.wō-stem*, [STOW *sb¹*];
  place 57

gestrangian, *w.v.(2)*, [STRONG];
  strengthen 190

gestrēon, *n.a-stem*, [I-STREON];
  profit 165

stunt, *adj.* [STUNT]; foolish,
  brute 250

sulh, syl (*dat.sg.*) 24; *f.monos-
  stem*, [SULLOW]; plough

sum, *indef.pron.,adj.* SOME 165;
  a 29

sumor, sumera (*dat.sg.*) 142;
  m.u-stem, SUMMER

GLOSSARY

sunnandæg, *m.a-stem,* SUNDAY 68

sunu, *m.u-stem,* SON 166

swā, *adv., conj.* SO 231 ; as 99 ; like 250 ; *swā s.* just as 214, like 257, as 296 ; *s. hwa s.* 81, *s. wylc s.* 102 whosoever ; *s. hwæðer . . . s. . . . s.* 240 whichever . . . whether . . . or

swæcc, *m.a-stem,* taste, flavour 181

swæs, *adj.* bland, suave 256

swefel, *m.a-stem,* sulphur 161

swēgincg, *f.ō-stem,* sound, clang, roar 227

swelgere, *m.ja-stem,* SWALLOWER ; glutton 292

swift, *adj.* SWIFT 64

swincgell, *f.ō-stem,* SWINGLE; stroke, stripe 10

swyftlēre, *m.i-stem,* slipper 171

swylc, *pron.* SUCH 108

swymman, *v.(3),* SWIM 102

swȳðe, *adv.* [SWITH] ; very, exceedingly 77 ; **swȳðost** *(sup.)* 65, especially

syfernys, *f.jō-stem,* moderation 296

sȳla, *m.n-stem,* ploughman 220

sylf, *pron.* SELF ; *hine sylfne (acc.)* 260, himself

syllan ; **sylle** *(1pres.sg.)* 81 ; **sylst** *(2pres.sg.)* 226 ; **sylð** *(3pres.sg.)* 83 ; **syle** *(imper.)* 136 ; *w.v.(1c),* SELL ; give

gesyllan, *w.v.(1c),* SELL ; 99

symble, *adv.* always 236

syn(n), *f.jō-stem,* SIN 314

syððan, *conj.* [SITHEN] ; after that 272

T

tǣcan, *w.v.(1c),* TEACH 1

temman 141, **temian** 131, 144, *w.v.(1a),* [TEME] ; tame

tīd, *f.i-stem,* [TIDE] ; canonical hour or service 14

getihtan, *w.v.(1b),* [TIGHT] ; incite, entice 57

tīma, *m.n-stem,* TIME 278

tin, *n.a-stem,* TIN 160

tō, *prep.(with dat.).* TO 24, for 95

tō, *adv.* TOO 188

tōdæg, *adv.* TODAY 67

tōforan, *prep.(with dat.),* [TOFORE] ; before 291

tōgēanes, *adv.* [TOGAINS] ; in the way 75

tōgelǣdan, *w.v.(1b),* bring, transport 155

tōgenȳdan, *w.v.(1b),* compel 10

tōgeȳcan, togehȳhte *(p.part. pl.)* 216 ; *w.v.(1b),* add

tōspecan, *v.(5),* address 203

tōwurpan, -on 234, *v.(3),* [TOWARP] ; dismiss, stop

trēowwyrhta, trȳw- 231 ; *m.n-stem,* carpenter 229

treppe, *f.n-stem,* TRAP 126

getrȳwe, *adj.* [I-TREOWE] ; faithful 42

twēgen, *num.* TWAIN, two 71

tweowa, *adv.* twice 40

tyddrian, *w.v.(2),* abound in, cherish 257

þ

þā, *adv.conj.* [THO] ; then 77 ; *þā þā* 268 when

þænne, see **þonne**

þær, *adv.* THERE 75, where 236

þæt, *conj.adv.* THAT 1

þancung, *f.ō-stem,* [THANKING] ; thanks 289

þanon, *adv.* [THENNE] ; whence 165, thence 120

þe, *rel.pron.* who, which, that 30 ; *se þ.* 239 he who

þe *(instrum.sg. of sē, þæt), adv.* ; *þ. lustlicor* 85, the more zealously ; *þ. læs conj* 39, lest

62

þēah, *conj.adv.* [THOUGH] ; yet 119

þēahhwæðere, *adv.* [THOUGH-WHETHER] ; moreover 202 ; nevertheless 15

geðeaht, *n.a-stem*, counsel, advice, 237

geðeahta, *m.n-stem*, counsellor 208

geðeahtend 224, -ynd 210 ; *m.a-stem*, counsellor

þéarle, *adv.* very, extremely 204 ; hard 23 ; ravenously 143

þēawlīce, *adv.* obediently 310 ; at attention 313

þencan, *w.v.*(*1c*), THINK, *v²* 256

þēof, *m.a-stem*, THIEF 46

þēowdōm, *m.a-stem*, [THEOW-DOM] ; service 213

þes, þæs 48 ; þēos (*f.nom.sg.*) 244 ; þis (*n.acc.sg.*) 237, þisse (*f.dat.sg.*) 268 ; þisum (*m.n. dat.sg.*) 155, þysum 271 ; þās (*nom.pl.*) 216, þisum (*dat.pl.*) 295 ; *dem. pron.* THIS

þīn, *adj.pron.* THINE 17

þing 250 ; þingc (*acc.pl.*) 154, etc., þincg 154, þing 247, þinc 158 ; þinga (*gen.pl.*) 157 ; *n.a-stem*, THING

þolian, *w.v.*(*2*), [THOLE] ; suffer 157

þonne, þænne 32, 44 ; *adv.conj.* THEN 163 ; THAN 8 ; when 44 ; yet, still 32

þræl, *m.a-stem*, THRALL 201

geðrīstian, *w.v.*(*2*), dare 121

þrȳste, *adj.* [THRISTE] ; bold, daring 77

þū, þē (*acc.*) 1, þīn (*gen.*) 175, þē (*dat.*) 211, 290 ; *pron.* THOU

þurhbrūcan, *v.*(*2*), enjoy to the full 180

þurhwerod, *adj.* very sweet 180

þus, *adv.* THUS 200

þusenthīwe, *adj.* shifty 255

geðwærian, *w.v.*(*2*), agree 236

geðwærnys, *f.jo-stem*, peace, concord 234

þylc, *pron.* [THELLICH] ; such 161

þync(e)an, *w.v.*(*1c*), *impers.* (*with dat.*), [THINK, *v¹*] ; appear, seem 211

þyrl, *n.a-stem*, [THIRL, *sb¹*] ; hole 232

þȳwan, *w.v.*(*1c*), urge, drive 24

U

ūhtsan(c)g, *m.a-stem*, UHT-SONG ; matins 270

unclǣne, *adj.* UNCLEAN 95 n

under, *prep.*(*with dat.*), UNDER 285

undertīd, *f.i-stem*, [UNDER-TIDE] ; tierce 272

understandan, *v.*(*6*), UNDER-STAND 247

underðēodan, *w.v.*(*1b*), subject, addicted to 257

unēaðe, *adv.*, [UNEATH] ; not easily, hardly 157

unforscēawodlīce, *adv.* unawares 59

ungelǣred, *adj.* illiterate, ignorant 2

unscennan, *w.v.*(*1b*), unyoke 45

ūt, *adv.* OUT 23

uton, see wītan

ūtwyrpan, *v.*(*3*), throw away 95

W

wacian, *w.v.*(*2*), WAKE ; watch 46

gewæmmodlīce, *adv.* corruptly, ungrammatically 2

wærlīce, *adv.* [WARELY] ; warily, circumspectly 280

wæter, *n.a-stem*, WATER 102

wæterian, *w.v.*(2), WATER 33

waxgeorn, *adj.* greedy 290

wĕ; ŭs (*acc.*) 219; ŭre (*gen.*) 209; ŭs (*dat.*) 225; *pron.* WE

wĕfod, *m.n.a-stem*, [WEVED]; altar 312

wel, *adv.* WELL 47, graciously 256

welig, *adj.*, [WEALY]; rich 151

weorc, geweorc 223, weorkes (*gen.sg.*) 12; *n.a-stem*, WORK; workmanship 223

wer, *m.a-stem*, [WERE, *sb*[1]]; man 191

wesan 243; wæs (*1.3sg.pret.*) 68; wære (*2sg.pret.*) 67; *v.*(5), be

wĭf, *n.a-stem*, WIFE 165

wĭkian, *w.v.*(2), [WICK, WIKE, *v*[1]]; dwell 225

wildĕor, [WILD DEER]; *n.a-stem*, wild animal 58

willan, *anom.v.* WILL, wish 7

wĭn, *n.a-stem*, WINE 160

winewinclan (*pl.*), *f.n-stem*, periwinkle 107

winter, wintra (*dat.sg.*) 138, *m.ɢ- stem*, WINTER 25

wĭs, *adj.* WISE 208; wĭsa (*w. form as voc.*) 211, wise man

wĭsdŏm, *m.a-stem*, WISDOM 254

wĭse, *f.n-stem*, [WISE, *sb*[1]]; way 124

gewĭslĭce, -wȳs- 32; *adv.* certainly, truly

wĭssian, *w.v.*(2), [WIS, *v*[1]]; instruct, guide 210

wĭtan, wăt (*3sg.pres.*) 283;

witaŏ (*3pl.pres.*), witun 9; *pret.-pres.*(1), [WIT, *v*[1]] know

wĭtan, *v.*(1), [WITE, *v*[2]]; go; uton (*1pl.subj.*) let us, 234

wiŏinnan, *adv.* WITHIN 257

witodlĭce, *adv.* truly, verily 168

wlĭĕtta, *m.n-stem*, [WLAT]; loathing 189

word, *n.a-stem*, WORD 256

woruldcrĭĕft, *m.a-stem*, secular occupation 217

wudu, *m.u-stem*, WOOD 139

wulf, *m.a-stem*, WOLF 39

gewuna, *m.n-stem*, [I-WUNE]; custom, practice 265

wunian, *w.v.*(2), [WON, WONE]; dwell 79

wynsum, *adj.* WINSOME 308

wyrcan, *w.v.*(1c), WORK; do 43; make 171

wyrhta, *m.n-stem*, WRIGHT, *sb*[1], workman 233

wyrt, *f.i-stem*, [WORT, *sb*[1]]; vegetable 288

wyrpan, *v.*(3), [WARP]; throw 92

wyrtgemangc, *n.a-stem*, mixture of herbs, spices, perfume 160

Y

yfele, *adv.* [EVIL]; evilly 256

ylpesbăn, *n.a-stem*, ivory 160

yppan, *w.v.*(1b), [UPPE]; reveal, betray 282

yrŏlin(c)g, 18, 226, -ngc- 22, *m.a-stem*, [EARTHLING, *sb*[1]]; ploughman 44